Just the Facts:
Earth and Space Science

by Jennifer Linrud Sinsel

Carson-Dellosa Publishing Company, Inc.
Greensboro, North Carolina

EDITOR: Matthew Fisher

LAYOUT DESIGN: Lori Jackson

INSIDE ILLUSTRATIONS: Don O'Connor

COVER DESIGN: Peggy Jackson

PHOTO CREDITS: © Photodisc
Photo courtesy of NASA

ISBN 978-1-59441-248-6

Just the Facts: Earth and Space Science

Just the Facts: Earth and Space Science

In 1994, geologists conducting research in Antarctica discovered a meteorite that was later determined to have come from Mars. While this find is amazing in itself, some scientists also think the meteorite may contain fossilized Martian bacteria!

Discovering possible evidence of past life on Mars requires the understanding of basic facts—the structure of bacteria, the atmospheric content of Mars, the gases contained in meteorites, elements commonly found in space, the processes involved in impact cratering, and how fossilization occurs. The list is seemingly endless. Without basic scientific knowledge, scientists would be unable to intelligently debate the prospect of discovering past life on Mars.

In *Just the Facts: Earth and Space Science*, students will be exposed to the basic factual knowledge that will allow them to conduct inquiry investigations, much like the experiments that real-world scientists conduct every day. The worksheets and activities in this book will supplement your daily lessons, and some can be used as stepping stones to full inquiry experiments that students can develop themselves.

The debate continues over whether or not Mars once contained life. Armed with scientific facts and knowledge, scientists carry on the process of inquiry and discovery. Perhaps one day, it will be one of your students who reveals the truth.

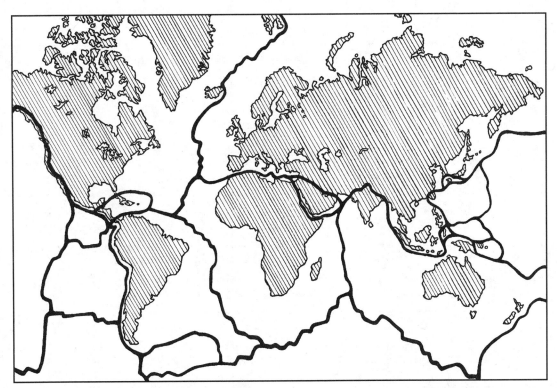

A = Science as Inquiry
B = Physical Science
C = Life Science

D = Earth and Space Science
E = Science and Technology

F = Science in Personal and Social Perspectives
G = History and Nature of Science

ACTIVITY	A	B	C	D	E	F	G
Scientists Who Study the Earth (page 9)				X		X	X
Elements in Earth's Crust (page 10)	X			X			
Meet the Minerals Word Search (page 11)				X			
Meet the Minerals Crossword Puzzle (page 12)				X			
Which Mineral Am I? (page 13)				X		X	
Mineral Matching (page 14)				X		X	
Minerals All around Us (page 15)				X		X	
Minerals Rock! (page 16)				X			
Magic Crystals (page 17)	X			X			
Igneous, Sedimentary, or Metamorphic? (page 19)				X			
Simply Sedimentary Crossword Puzzle (page 20)				X			
The Pressure on Metamorphic Rocks (page 21)				X			
Which Rock Am I? (page 22)				X		X	
The Rock Cycle (page 23)				X		X	
A "Rock"-ing Autobiography (page 24)	X			X		X	
Modeling Rocks (page 25)	X			X			
The Weathering of Earth Word Search (page 27)				X			
The Weathering of Earth Crossword Puzzle (page 28)				X			
Mechanical or Chemical? (page 29)				X			
Mechanical Weathering (page 30)	X	X		X			
What's in Our Soil? (page 32)				X			
Over the Horizon (page 33)				X			
Fascinating Fossils Word Search (page 34)			X	X			
Fascinating Fossils Crossword Puzzle (page 35)			X	X			
Unconformities (page 36)				X			
Layers of Rock (page 37)				X			
Millions of Years Ago . . . (page 38)	X		X	X			
A Paleontology Puzzle (page 40)	X		X	X		X	X
Earth's Shifting Surface Word Search (page 42)				X			
Earth's Shifting Surface Crossword Puzzle (page 43)				X			
The Puzzle of Pangaea (page 44)	X			X			
A Controversial Idea (page 45)	X			X		X	X
Know Your Boundaries (page 46)				X			
Inside the Earth (page 47)				X			
A Current Event (page 48)	X	X		X			
Quaking, Shaking Earth Word Search (page 49)				X		X	
Quaking, Shaking Earth Crossword Puzzle (page 50)				X		X	
Earthquake Travel Times (page 51)	X			X		X	
Earthquake Locations (page 52)				X		X	
Whose "Fault" Is It? (page 54)				X		X	
Quaking Elsewhere! (page 55)	X			X			
Shakedown! (page 56)	X	X		X	X	X	
Earth's Cooling Vents Word Search (page 58)				X			
Earth's Cooling Vents Crossword Puzzle (page 59)				X			
Flowing Eruptions (page 60)				X			
Movement inside the Earth (page 61)				X			

ACTIVITY	A	B	C	D	E	F	G
Otherworldly Volcanoes (page 62)	X			X			
Lava in the Lab—Part 1 (page 63)	X	X		X		X	
Lava in the Lab—Part 2 (page 65)	X	X		X		X	
A Cycle of Water (page 66)				X			
Rivers and Streams Word Search (page 67)				X			
Rivers and Streams Crossword Puzzle (page 68)				X			
The Groundwater Shuffle (page 69)				X			
Stream Stages (page 70)				X			
Speeding Streams and Rivers—Part 1 (page 71)	X	X		X			
Speeding Streams and Rivers—Part 2 (page 72)	X	X		X			
The Life and Times of a Water Droplet (page 73)	X			X			
The Living Ocean Word Search (page 74)			X	X		X	
The Living Ocean Crossword Puzzle (page 75)			X	X		X	
Waves and Tides (page 76)				X			
The Ocean Floor (page 77)				X			
Ocean Life Poster (page 78)	X		X	X			
Ocean Pollution (page 80)			X	X		X	
Do the Wave! (page 81)	X	X		X		X	
Earth's Protective Blanket Word Search (page 82)				X			
Earth's Protective Blanket Crossword Puzzle (page 83)				X			
Way Up in the Sky (page 84)				X			
Graphing the Atmosphere (page 85)	X			X			
Is the Earth Heating Up? (page 86)	X			X		X	X
Under Pressure! (page 87)	X	X		X			
Screening the Sun (page 89)	X	X		X		X	
Patterns of Weather Word Search (page 91)				X			
Patterns of Weather Crossword Puzzle (page 92)				X			
Fronts (page 93)				X			
Station Models (page 94)				X			
Climactic Clues Crossword Puzzle (page 96)				X			
In the Zone (page 97)			X	X			
Global Climates (page 98)	X	X		X			
The Fragile Environment Word Search (page 99)				X		X	
The Fragile Environment Crossword Puzzle (page 100)				X		X	
A Fair Share of Resources? (page 101)	X			X		X	
Alternative Resources (page 102)				X		X	
An Energy Alternative (page 103)	X			X		X	
Sources of Air Pollution (page 104)				X		X	
Is Your Rain Acidic? (page 105)	X			X		X	
Our Home Planet Earth Crossword Puzzle (page 107)				X		X	
Earth's Satellite Word Search (page 108)				X			
Earth's Satellite Crossword Puzzle (page 109)				X			
Sun-Earth-Moon System (page 110)				X			
To the Moon! (page 111)				X	X	X	X
Solar and Lunar Eclipses (page 112)				X		X	
Modeling Moon Phases (page 114)	X			X		X	
Our Solar System Word Search (page 115)				X			
Inner Solar System Crossword Puzzle (page 116)				X			
Outer Solar System Crossword Puzzle (page 117)				X			
Solar System Distances (page 118)				X			
Which Planet Am I? (page 119)				X			
Planetary Missions (page 120)	X			X	X	X	X

Show What You Know!

DIRECTIONS: Before you begin learning about this topic, complete the first three sections of the **KWL** chart below. Under **K**, list what you already know about the topic. Under **W**, list what you would like to find out about the topic. Once you have studied the topic, come back to the chart and list what you learned under **L**.

TOPIC: _____

K What I Know	W What I Want to Know	L What I Have Learned

INTRODUCTION

Scientists Who Study the Earth

FILL IN THE BLANKS

No one scientist could know everything about the entire Earth—it is too large of a place! Scientists who are interested in studying the earth specialize in one specific area, such as rocks or earthquakes. These scientists go to school for many years to become experts in their fields. They also write reports that are often published in scientific journals. What kind of Earth scientist would you like to be?

DIRECTIONS: Write each type of Earth scientist in the correct blank below to match the scientists with the topics they study.

WORD BANK

volcanologist	planetary geologist	geochemist
cartographer	gemologist	climatologist
petroleum geologist	meteorologist	seismologist
paleontologist	hydrogeologist	oceanographer

1. earthquakes and seismic activity _____

2. weather patterns _____

3. the rocks, soil, and structures found in the ocean _____

4. fossils, past life forms, and ancient climates _____

5. maps and the layout of Earth's physical features, such as continents _____

6. gems, such as rubies and diamonds _____

7. water found in the earth _____

8. active and extinct volcanoes _____

9. chemical makeup of rocks _____

10. rocks on other planets _____

11. present-day and past climates _____

12. oil or gas that is below the surface of the earth _____

Name: _____ Date: _____

Elements in Earth's Crust

There are **92 elements** that occur naturally on the planet Earth. These 92 elements combine to make everything you see around you, such as rocks, trees, ducks, and cars. Eight common elements in rocks make up Earth's crust. Of these eight, the two most abundant, **oxygen** and **silicon**, combine to make silicates. **Silicates** are types of minerals. Many minerals fall into the silicate category, including quartz, mica, and feldspar.

DIRECTIONS: The eight most common elements in Earth's crust are listed below by percentage. On the blank graph below, create a bar graph using this data. Then, answer the questions that follow.

Name of Element	Symbol	Percentage of Crust
oxygen	O	46.6 %
silicon	Si	27.7 %
aluminum	Al	8.1 %
iron	Fe	5.0 %
calcium	Ca	3.6 %
sodium	Na	2.8 %
potassium	K	2.6 %
magnesium	Mg	2.1 %

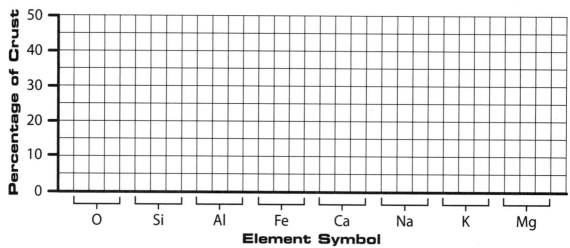

1. What percentage of Earth's crust is made up of the eight most common elements? _____

2. What percentage is made up of other elements? _____

3. What percentage of Earth's crust is made up of oxygen and silicon? _____

Meet the Minerals

WORD SEARCH

DIRECTIONS: Find the minerals vocabulary words in the word search below. Words can be found across, down, and diagonally. Then, on a separate piece of paper, write sentences for five of the words.

WORD BANK

sulfur	color	streak	mica	Mohs scale
pyrite	halite	luster	cleavage	fracture
calcite	magnetite	talc	ore	gems
graphite	quartz	hardness	crystal	mineral

```
C  I  P  L  I  Z  A  J  P  P  O  H  I  O  Q  O  A  J  Q  V
L  A  F  M  F  X  W  H  G  F  C  S  A  U  X  B  C  Y  B  O
E  K  X  O  R  W  X  R  O  S  A  U  E  R  U  T  C  V  B  U
A  I  P  H  A  K  R  U  Q  P  L  L  T  K  D  E  A  Q  N  M
V  K  Y  S  C  Q  Q  K  C  X  C  F  N  L  V  N  A  L  D  X
A  B  R  S  T  U  H  R  M  U  I  U  W  T  U  X  E  X  C  D
G  Q  I  C  U  A  W  T  M  P  T  R  L  Y  H  S  E  S  N  E
E  E  T  A  R  R  V  U  R  A  E  L  L  O  R  E  T  N  S  V
A  W  E  L  E  T  P  I  L  N  G  B  I  N  N  P  T  E  V  Q
U  G  Q  E  U  Z  B  S  I  D  A  N  H  T  N  T  Y  Y  R  M
W  N  Y  C  E  C  S  U  D  K  S  G  E  V  V  B  E  V  Y  K
Y  O  A  R  S  T  R  E  A  K  R  K  S  T  M  T  W  G  Y  I
M  X  U  Y  J  H  E  M  I  N  E  R  A  L  I  Z  X  T  Q  B
R  I  H  S  O  Q  A  F  M  Z  Q  S  G  H  C  T  A  P  V  D
P  T  P  T  F  L  G  L  D  Z  E  S  P  O  A  R  E  H  P  G
Q  D  T  A  C  I  E  V  I  P  C  A  C  L  K  O  B  E  C  E
N  I  M  L  Z  T  M  M  I  T  R  R  Z  B  Y  E  R  B  O  X
Q  E  C  U  M  P  S  N  K  G  E  X  R  J  B  O  A  I  L  X
A  S  B  E  L  H  T  G  W  N  L  A  X  U  L  P  S  I  O  G
Z  V  H  F  J  L  X  H  A  A  B  R  G  X  K  C  E  E  R  W
```

Meet the Minerals

DIRECTIONS: Complete the crossword puzzle.

ACROSS

3. the least accurate way to identify a mineral

4. mineral with glassy luster, often clear or milky white

8. mineral whose common name is salt

9. A test for this mineral consists of pouring acid over the mineral.

12. describes how minerals break

13. fool's gold

14. the way light reflects off the surface of a mineral

DOWN

1. mineral used in pencils

2. magnetic mineral

5. mineral with silky luster that is used in baby powder

6. flat mineral with flaky cleavage

7. yellow mineral that smells like burnt matches

10. determined by using a fingernail, penny, or nail

11. the color of the powder that is left when a mineral is rubbed across a porcelain plate

Name: _____ Date: _____

Which Mineral Am I?

DIRECTIONS: Read the clues that describe a type of mineral. Write the name of the mineral from the word bank on the line below its matching set of clues.

WORD BANK

quartz	galena	graphite
talc	sulfur	magnetite

1. I am a yellow mineral.
   My hardness is 2.
   My streak is yellow.
   Some people say that I smell like burnt matches or rotten eggs.

   Which mineral am I?

   _____

2. I am a dark gray mineral.
   My hardness is 1.
   My streak is dark gray, and my luster is greasy.
   I am used in pencil lead.

   Which mineral am I?

   _____

3. I may contain silver.
   My cleavage is cubic.
   My streak is black or dark gray.
   My luster is metallic.

   Which mineral am I?

   _____

4. I am a mineral that can be many different colors.
   My hardness is 7.
   My streak is white.
   I am a common mineral in sand.

   Which mineral am I?

   _____

5. I am a gray, brownish-red, or black mineral.
   My hardness is 6–7.
   My streak is black.
   I am attracted to a magnet.

   Which mineral am I?

   _____

6. I am a white or light gray mineral.
   My hardness is 1.
   My streak is white.
   I am smooth to the touch, like soap.

   Which mineral am I?

   _____

Mineral Matching

M Y S T E R Y   W O R D

Many of the objects that you use every day are created from **minerals**. The minerals that we mine from the earth help us perform many daily tasks and make our lives easier. Imagine what life might be like if we did not have some of these objects. If we did not have electrical wiring, we would not have electrical switches in our homes or schools. Without cement, our roads and sidewalks would not be usable for driving cars or riding bicycles.

DIRECTIONS: Write each letter in the correct blank to match each mineral to its common use. Within the answers of the first column, there is a hidden mystery vocabulary word. Use the clue at the bottom of the page to help you find it.

Name of Mineral

1. _____ halite
2. _____ mica
3. _____ quartz
4. _____ silver
5. _____ talc
6. _____ graphite
7. _____ calcite
8. _____ chalcopyrite (copper ore)
9. _____ gypsum
10. _____ sulfur
11. _____ feldspar
12. _____ mercury
13. _____ chromium
14. _____ uranium

Common Use

a. baby powder
b. glass
c. pencil lead
d. electrical wiring
e. fireworks
f. paint
g. food seasoning
h. jewelry
i. chalk
j. thermometers
k. atomic energy
l. plaster and cement
m. porcelain sinks
n. car bumpers

MYSTERY WORD: This substance will fizz when placed on a calcite mineral.

____ ____ ____ ____

Name: _____ Date: _____

Igneous, Sedimentary, or Metamorphic?

The rocks that make up Earth's crust are constantly changing over time. Rocks can form in several ways, and each type of rock forms by a different process.

Sedimentary rocks are formed by cementation or compaction of sediments. Most sedimentary rocks are made of materials that have been moved from their original places by water, wind, waves, or ice. Sedimentary rocks form in layers over millions of years and may contain fossils.

Metamorphic rocks are formed by intense heat and pressure. All kinds of rocks—sedimentary, igneous, and metamorphic rocks—can be changed by this process. These rocks are created by the heat and pressure from the weight of Earth's crust bearing down from above.

Igneous rocks are formed by melting and crystallization. These rocks are created when hot liquids and gases inside Earth's mantle cool or when hot magma rises and melts other types of rocks in Earth's crust.

DIRECTIONS: Use a dictionary, science book, or the Internet to help you label each type of rock. In each blank, write *S* for sedimentary, *M* for metamorphic, or *I* for igneous.

1. gneiss _____

2. siltstone _____

3. limestone _____

4. granite _____

5. conglomerate _____

6. obsidian _____

7. rhyolite _____

8. schist _____

9. shale _____

10. marble _____

11. sandstone _____

12. basalt _____

13. pumice _____

14. slate _____

15. breccia _____

16. halite _____

17. gabbro _____

18. quartzite _____

19. flint _____

20. tuff _____

Name: _____ Date: _____

Simply Sedimentary

CROSSWORD PUZZLE

DIRECTIONS: Complete the crossword puzzle.

ACROSS

1. type of sedimentary rock that forms when sediments stick together

3. type of sedimentary rock that forms when minerals crystallize out of a solution

4. the breakdown of rock into smaller sediments, beginning the process of sedimentary rock formation

6. type of sedimentary rock that forms from the remains of organisms

8. a coarse-grained sedimentary rock in which large, rounded sediments can be seen

9. rock that forms when sediments are cemented or compacted together

10. a fine-grained sedimentary rock that forms slate when placed under extreme heat and pressure

DOWN

1. the process by which sediments are stuck together to form sedimentary rock

2. term for the layering of sedimentary rock

3. the process by which sediments are pushed together in layers to form sedimentary rock

5. remains of plants and animals that have been preserved in sedimentary rock

7. a sedimentary rock that forms from calcium carbonate and fizzes in acid

Modeling Rocks

I N Q U I R Y   I N V E S T I G A T I O N

Sedimentary rocks are formed by cementation or compaction of sediments. Most sedimentary rocks are made of materials that have been moved from their original places by water, wind, waves, or ice. Sedimentary rocks form in layers over millions of years and may contain fossils.

Metamorphic rocks are formed by intense heat and pressure. All kinds of rocks—sedimentary, igneous, and metamorphic rocks—can be changed by this process. These rocks are created by the heat and pressure from the weight of Earth's crust bearing down from above.

Igneous rocks are formed by melting and crystallization. These rocks are created when hot liquids and gases inside Earth's mantle cool or when hot magma rises and melts other types of rocks in Earth's crust.

DIRECTIONS: You will model the rock cycle using several pieces of clay. Follow the procedure as you begin with one type of rock and change it into the other types of rocks.

M A T E R I A L S

three balls of different colors of clay	piece of newspaper	colorful pencils

PROCEDURE:

1. Place a piece of newspaper on a table to work on. Choose one ball of colorful clay and divide it into two equal pieces. Flatten each piece into a round disc.

2. Tear off small pieces from the other two balls of clay and roll them into tiny balls. Place these tiny balls of colorful clay on top of one of the flat pieces. Place the other flat piece on top of the clay balls. The model rock should look like this:

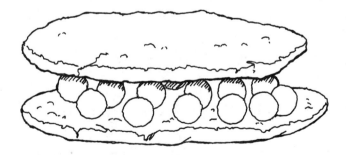

3. Color the picture above so that it looks like the model. What type of rock have you created?

_____

4. Press down hard on the model rock with your fist. Fold the rock in half and press down hard again. Draw and color a picture of the rock in the space below.

5. What type of rock have you created?

_____

6. Put the model rock between both hands and knead it for several minutes. As you knead the clay, it should begin to feel warm. This represents the melting that rocks undergo when they are below Earth's crust. After a time, you may not be able to distinguish one color of clay from another. Draw and color a picture of the rock in the space below.

7. What type of rock have you created?

_____

CONCLUSION:

8. How is this process similar to the rock cycle? How is it different?

_____

_____

_____

Name: _____   Date: _____

The Weathering of Earth

DIRECTIONS: Find the weathering vocabulary words in the word search puzzle below. Words can be found across, down, and diagonally. Then, on a separate piece of paper, write sentences for five of the words.

WORD BANK

abrasion	gravity	roots
acid rain	ice wedging	water
chemical	mechanical	weathering
differential	oxidation	wind

```
J  I  I  P  D  L  K  R  W  J  V  I  D  C  M  Z  C  Z  W  P
A  F  X  V  F  H  M  J  R  T  R  M  F  U  L  J  I  Q  Z  C
H  Q  R  I  O  K  M  E  Z  J  C  J  G  V  P  D  E  E  F  H
Z  B  O  M  N  R  T  A  O  X  I  D  A  T  I  O  N  Y  W  E
W  D  D  T  E  A  T  Q  C  K  E  W  P  C  C  J  J  V  W  M
M  I  Z  I  W  C  N  P  F  Q  P  M  Z  H  Y  B  M  M  P  I
P  F  N  F  N  Q  H  F  O  R  R  S  Q  L  Z  W  Y  P  I  C
G  F  I  D  N  H  W  A  X  R  W  B  R  H  T  E  D  P  W  A
N  E  L  Z  V  A  W  K  N  F  E  A  B  R  A  S  I  O  N  L
Y  R  I  C  E  W  E  D  G  I  N  G  W  J  N  B  K  Y  G  B
Q  E  V  N  K  B  Q  X  P  L  C  D  S  I  Q  C  S  N  M  F
P  N  P  I  G  T  G  P  R  X  W  A  A  Q  I  Y  I  A  O  B
R  T  Q  V  N  X  R  G  H  A  I  R  L  P  O  R  C  L  N  M
X  I  L  Z  W  L  A  G  E  D  D  R  V  P  E  S  M  K  C  G
K  A  Q  J  E  M  V  V  R  I  K  L  R  H  O  H  I  R  P  T
T  L  F  U  U  X  I  E  C  G  R  V  T  X  L  D  R  O  K  D
M  X  P  T  A  L  T  A  N  O  Z  A  X  Q  M  R  U  O  F  K
U  D  I  U  H  J  Y  M  O  I  E  N  Q  P  T  J  X  T  X  Q
E  O  T  N  Q  R  F  U  N  W  P  R  I  H  C  O  O  S  O  A
Z  B  Z  A  K  L  B  G  R  G  B  F  M  U  H  A  J  X  Y  M
```

Name: _____ Date: _____

The Weathering of Earth

CROSSWORD PUZZLE

DIRECTIONS: Complete the crossword puzzle.

ACROSS

2. the breakdown of rock into smaller pieces

4. a chemical reaction in which metal combines with oxygen to form rust

7. Landslides are a form of mechanical weathering caused by the force of _____ .

8. _____ weathering is the breakdown of a rock's minerals by water, oxygen, carbon dioxide, living organisms, and acid rain.

9. caused when water in the cracks in rocks freezes and expands

11. causes mechanical weathering by blowing sand against exposed rock

12. Plant _____ can grow into existing cracks in rocks and cause mechanical weathering.

DOWN

1. _____ weathering is a process by which softer, less weather-resistant rocks are worn away, leaving more weather-resistant rocks exposed.

3. can be found in polluted rainwater; causes chemical weathering

5. the action of rocks grinding against each other and wearing away exposed surfaces

6. _____ weathering is the breakdown of a rock into smaller pieces by freezing, thawing, plant growth, or the actions of animals.

10. element of nature that can cause mechanical weathering by flowing over or carrying rocks along in a current

Name: _____ Date: _____

Mechanical or Chemical?

There are two types of weathering—mechanical and chemical. **Mechanical weathering** is when a rock is physically broken into smaller pieces. The rock's chemical composition does not change. **Chemical weathering** is when a rock breaks down through a chemical change by water, air, or other substances. The minerals in the rock are changed into new materials.

DIRECTIONS: Decide if each situation below describes mechanical or chemical weathering. Write *M* for mechanical or *C* for chemical in each blank. Then, draw examples of the two types of weathering in the boxes below.

1. _____ Limestone is dissolved by acid rain.

2. _____ A large rock falls from a cliff and breaks.

3. _____ Water in the cracks of a rock freezes and breaks apart the rock.

4. _____ An old car sitting outside for several years forms rust on its underside.

5. _____ Tree roots crack the foundation of a house.

6. _____ Moss grows on the surface of a rock, producing pits.

7. _____ A rock is carried along the bottom of a stream causing its edges to round over a period of time.

8. _____ A marble gravestone becomes difficult to read over time in an area with high pollution.

9. _____ Wind blows sand against a rock formation in the desert.

10. _____ A gopher burrows through coarse sediment and brings it to the surface.

Mechanical Weathering	Chemical Weathering

WEATHERING

Mechanical Weathering

INQUIRY INVESTIGATION

Weathering is the breakdown of rock into smaller and smaller pieces. It can take place over long or short periods of time and by mechanical or chemical means. How does mechanical weathering affect the mass of rock? The following experiment will help demonstrate the mechanical process of weathering.

MATERIALS

sample of limestone or sandstone	plastic bottle or jar with a lid	stopwatch or clock
	balance or scale	paper towels
water	beaker	

PROCEDURE:

1. Place the sample of rock in the tray of the balance. Find the mass of the rock. Record the mass in the data table below in the space marked 0 minutes.

2. Fill the plastic bottle $\frac{1}{3}$ full of water. Place the sample of rock in the bottle. Seal the bottle tightly with the lid.

3. Shake the bottle for two minutes.

4. Pour the water from the bottle into the beaker. Remove the rock from the bottle. Use the paper towel to gently pat the rock dry.

5. Place the rock on the tray of the balance. Find the mass of the rock. Record the mass in the data table.

6. Repeat steps 2–5 nine more times (for a total of 20 minutes).

DATA TABLE:

	Time (minutes)										
	0	2	4	6	8	10	12	14	16	18	20
Mass of Rock (g)											

RESULTS:

1. How did the mass of the rock change throughout the experiment?

   _____

   _____

2. What was the total change in the mass of the rock from the beginning to the end of the experiment?

_____

CONCLUSIONS:

3. Why did the mass of the rock change from the beginning to the end of the experiment?

_____

_____

_____

4. How does this experiment model an event that occurs naturally?

_____

_____

_____

5. Create a line graph using the data collected in this experiment.

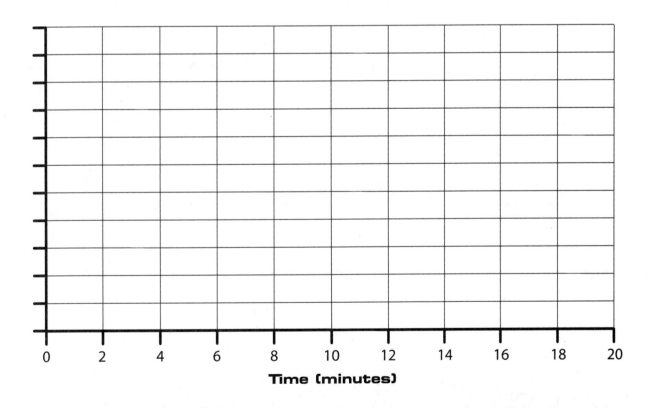

What's in Our Soil?

M A G I C   N U M B E R

DIRECTIONS: Write each letter in the correct blank to match each vocabulary term with its definition. Then, copy the number of each answer into the box below with the matching letter. When you add the numbers down, across, and diagonally, the sums should be the same.

1. _____ humus

2. _____ soil profile

3. _____ horizon C

4. _____ litter

5. _____ horizon B

6. _____ soil

7. _____ horizon A

8. _____ climate

9. _____ leaching

a. All horizons of a soil together form a _____.

b. the removal of minerals from soil from being dissolved in water

c. _____ consists of leaves, twigs, and other organic material that eventually decay and change into humus.

d. top layer of soil in a soil profile; made of topsoil

e. layer directly below horizon A; made of humus, clay, and other minerals

f. the bottom horizon in a soil profile; contains only partly weathered rock

g. mixture of rock particles, decayed organic matter, minerals, water, and air

h. dark-colored decayed organic matter found in soil

i. pattern of weather that occurs in an area over a long period of time and can affect the type of soil in that area

a.	b.	c.
d.	e.	f.
g.	h.	i.

MAGIC NUMBER = _____

Over the Horizon

DIRECTIONS: Write each term from the word bank in the correct blank to label the layers of the soil profile. Then, write the name of each soil layer next to its correct description below. Some terms will be used more than once.

W O R D   B A N K

horizon O (humus)	horizon R (bedrock)	horizon C
horizon B	horizon A	

1. _____

2. _____

3. _____

4. _____

5. _____

6. _____ Materials that are leached from horizon A are deposited into this horizon.

7. _____ This horizon is composed of unweathered bedrock.

8. _____ This horizon contains large pieces of broken-up bedrock.

9. _____ This horizon is also known as topsoil.

10. _____ This horizon is lighter in color than horizon A since it is mostly clay and contains little humus.

11. _____ A soil profile with a thin amount of this horizon would not be able to support the growth of many plants.

12. _____ This top organic layer of soil contains leaf litter and humus.

Fascinating Fossils

DIRECTIONS: Find the fossil vocabulary words in the word search puzzle below. Words can be found across, down, and diagonally. Then, on a separate piece of paper, write sentences for five of the words.

WORD BANK

amber	crinoid	index fossil	mosquito	trace fossil
carbon	dinosaur	mammoth	permineralization	trilobite
cast	fossil	mold	petrified	

```
K  X  V  G  V  Z  T  C  W  K  N  E  Q  O  L  A  J  L  I  C
Z  A  V  X  A  I  N  R  L  J  J  W  Q  Y  Q  O  K  D  O  P
P  D  R  L  L  K  I  Z  B  I  G  T  Q  U  P  H  F  I  B  L
Y  I  P  U  E  G  I  X  E  S  H  I  X  F  C  Z  E  I  P  S
S  N  C  E  E  F  T  X  M  G  U  C  L  N  A  X  I  D  E  C
T  O  T  R  T  I  G  A  X  F  A  F  J  Q  R  Q  W  T  R  T
C  S  R  F  I  R  T  X  W  A  J  M  I  T  B  O  X  R  M  Q
M  A  I  E  W  N  I  E  O  Q  C  U  B  G  O  F  G  A  I  H
O  U  L  D  G  Q  O  F  I  R  C  E  L  E  N  G  F  C  N  K
L  R  O  W  J  T  S  I  I  W  Y  Z  E  I  R  D  J  E  E  M
D  H  B  K  O  F  I  N  D  E  X  F  O  S  S  I  L  F  R  B
C  U  I  N  U  B  F  G  S  M  D  C  X  H  J  S  O  O  A  O
K  K  T  F  M  P  L  K  T  M  E  E  A  U  C  I  Q  S  L  N
H  I  E  O  O  R  Y  E  K  A  E  R  S  S  W  H  G  S  I  G
D  T  D  B  J  S  Z  L  V  M  O  U  S  O  T  E  X  I  Z  A
L  A  E  O  N  Z  S  K  G  M  A  C  R  Z  V  E  G  L  A  L
I  K  B  X  B  V  F  I  D  O  V  M  D  G  E  S  T  E  T  P
Z  E  W  B  N  I  T  W  L  T  K  F  E  K  S  H  B  H  I  D
J  B  I  X  B  A  V  M  V  H  X  V  K  O  Z  W  K  O  O  M
Z  Y  X  O  H  G  S  M  O  S  Q  U  I  T  O  B  T  N  N  V
```

Name: _____   Date: _____

Fascinating Fossils

CROSSWORD PUZZLE

DIRECTIONS: Complete the crossword puzzle.

ACROSS

2. an empty cavity in rock where a plant or animal was buried

4. _____ fossils are the remains of species that existed abundantly on Earth for relatively short periods of time in widespread areas.

8. process in which minerals fill in pore spaces of an organism's tissues

9. hardened tree sap in which preserved insects can sometimes be found

DOWN

1. remains, imprints, or traces of naturally preserved organisms

3. describes an organism whose tissues are completely replaced by minerals

5. A _____ fossil is preserved evidence of animal activity, such as a track or burrow.

6. an object created when minerals and sediment fill a mold, creating an exact copy of the buried organism

7. The isotope of _____–14 is useful for dating bones, wood, and charcoal up to 75,000 years old.

Unconformities

An **unconformity** is a rock surface that represents a missing part of the geologic record. In studying unconformities, geologists place them into three separate categories: **disconformities**, **nonconformities**, and **angular unconformities**.

DIRECTIONS: Write each letter in the correct blank to match the type of unconformity with its definition. Then, label each rock diagram below as a *disconformity*, a *nonconformity*, or an *angular unconformity*.

1. _____ nonconformity

2. _____ disconformity

3. _____ angular unconformity

a. Younger layers of sedimentary rock lie on top of older layers of flat-lying sedimentary rock, which show signs of erosion by wind, water, or ice.

b. Sedimentary rock layers lie on top of an eroded surface of igneous or metamorphic rock.

c. Rock layers, found below a layer of younger sedimentary rock, appear to be tilted or folded.

4. _____

5. _____

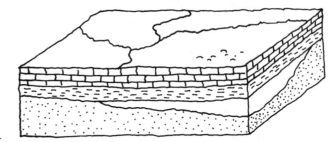

6. _____

Layers of Rock

Like the layers in a cake, sediments are layered in the order in which they were deposited. This is called the **principle of superposition**. Scientists can study a **cross section** or **core samples** from an area and determine which types of rocks are the oldest and which are the youngest. When fossils are uncovered, their ages can often be determined based upon the rock layer in which they are found.

DIRECTIONS: Look at the cross sections of the rock layers below. Determine the order in which the rock layers were deposited, from oldest to youngest, and write the letters in the correct blanks.

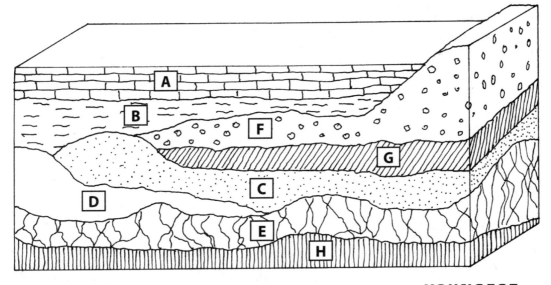

OLDEST ___ ___ ___ ___ ___ ___ ___ ___ **YOUNGEST**

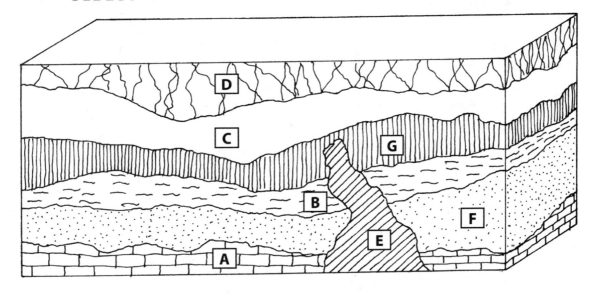

OLDEST ___ ___ ___ ___ ___ ___ ___ **YOUNGEST**

FOSSILS

Millions of Years Ago . . .

MATH SKILLS

Geologic time is often hard to visualize. Earth's history spans many millions of years, but exactly what does one million look like? One million is a pretty big number. Since the geologic time scale is divided into periods that are millions of years in length, it can be difficult to understand the vast amount of time involved.

DIRECTIONS: Use page 39 to help you answer and visualize the solution for each problem. Use the space below each problem to show your work.

1. To help you visualize what a million looks like, look at page 39. It is covered with the letter *x*. There are approximately 3,300 *X*s on the page. How many pages would you need for 1,000,000 *X*s? Use the space below to show your work.

   Answer: _____

2. Dinosaurs died out near the end of the Cretaceous Period 65 million years ago. How many pages would you need to show 65 million *X*s?

   Answer: _____

3. Trilobites are extinct organisms with hard outer skeletons that lived during different periods. The Cambrian Period, during which Trilobites first appeared, lasted about 39 million years. How many pages would you need to show 39 million *X*s?

   Answer: _____

4. Trilobites inhabited Earth's oceans for more than 200 million years. How many pages would you need to show 200 million *X*s?

   Answer: _____

XXXXXXXXXXXXXXXXXXXXXXXXXXXXXXXXXXXXXXXXXXXXXXXXXXXXXXXX
XXXXXXXXXXXXXXXXXXXXXXXXXXXXXXXXXXXXXXXXXXXXXXXXXXXXXXXX
XXXXXXXXXXXXXXXXXXXXXXXXXXXXXXXXXXXXXXXXXXXXXXXXXXXXXXXX
XXXXXXXXXXXXXXXXXXXXXXXXXXXXXXXXXXXXXXXXXXXXXXXXXXXXXXXX
XXXXXXXXXXXXXXXXXXXXXXXXXXXXXXXXXXXXXXXXXXXXXXXXXXXXXXXX
XXXXXXXXXXXXXXXXXXXXXXXXXXXXXXXXXXXXXXXXXXXXXXXXXXXXXXXX
XXXXXXXXXXXXXXXXXXXXXXXXXXXXXXXXXXXXXXXXXXXXXXXXXXXXXXXX
XXXXXXXXXXXXXXXXXXXXXXXXXXXXXXXXXXXXXXXXXXXXXXXXXXXXXXXX
XXXXXXXXXXXXXXXXXXXXXXXXXXXXXXXXXXXXXXXXXXXXXXXXXXXXXXXX
XXXXXXXXXXXXXXXXXXXXXXXXXXXXXXXXXXXXXXXXXXXXXXXXXXXXXXXX
XXXXXXXXXXXXXXXXXXXXXXXXXXXXXXXXXXXXXXXXXXXXXXXXXXXXXXXX
XXXXXXXXXXXXXXXXXXXXXXXXXXXXXXXXXXXXXXXXXXXXXXXXXXXXXXXX
XXXXXXXXXXXXXXXXXXXXXXXXXXXXXXXXXXXXXXXXXXXXXXXXXXXXXXXX
XXXXXXXXXXXXXXXXXXXXXXXXXXXXXXXXXXXXXXXXXXXXXXXXXXXXXXXX
XXXXXXXXXXXXXXXXXXXXXXXXXXXXXXXXXXXXXXXXXXXXXXXXXXXXXXXX
XXXXXXXXXXXXXXXXXXXXXXXXXXXXXXXXXXXXXXXXXXXXXXXXXXXXXXXX
XXXXXXXXXXXXXXXXXXXXXXXXXXXXXXXXXXXXXXXXXXXXXXXXXXXXXXXX
XXXXXXXXXXXXXXXXXXXXXXXXXXXXXXXXXXXXXXXXXXXXXXXXXXXXXXXX
XXXXXXXXXXXXXXXXXXXXXXXXXXXXXXXXXXXXXXXXXXXXXXXXXXXXXXXX
XXXXXXXXXXXXXXXXXXXXXXXXXXXXXXXXXXXXXXXXXXXXXXXXXXXXXXXX
XXXXXXXXXXXXXXXXXXXXXXXXXXXXXXXXXXXXXXXXXXXXXXXXXXXXXXXX
XXXXXXXXXXXXXXXXXXXXXXXXXXXXXXXXXXXXXXXXXXXXXXXXXXXXXXXX
XXXXXXXXXXXXXXXXXXXXXXXXXXXXXXXXXXXXXXXXXXXXXXXXXXXXXXXX
XXXXXXXXXXXXXXXXXXXXXXXXXXXXXXXXXXXXXXXXXXXXXXXXXXXXXXXX
XXXXXXXXXXXXXXXXXXXXXXXXXXXXXXXXXXXXXXXXXXXXXXXXXXXXXXXX
XXXXXXXXXXXXXXXXXXXXXXXXXXXXXXXXXXXXXXXXXXXXXXXXXXXXXXXX
XXXXXXXXXXXXXXXXXXXXXXXXXXXXXXXXXXXXXXXXXXXXXXXXXXXXXXXX
XXXXXXXXXXXXXXXXXXXXXXXXXXXXXXXXXXXXXXXXXXXXXXXXXXXXXXXX
XXXXXXXXXXXXXXXXXXXXXXXXXXXXXXXXXXXXXXXXXXXXXXXXXXXXXXXX
XXXXXXXXXXXXXXXXXXXXXXXXXXXXXXXXXXXXXXXXXXXXXXXXXXXXXXXX
XXXXXXXXXXXXXXXXXXXXXXXXXXXXXXXXXXXXXXXXXXXXXXXXXXXXXXXX
XXXXXXXXXXXXXXXXXXXXXXXXXXXXXXXXXXXXXXXXXXXXXXXXXXXXXXXX
XXXXXXXXXXXXXXXXXXXXXXXXXXXXXXXXXXXXXXXXXXXXXXXXXXXXXXXX

A Paleontology Puzzle

A **paleontologist** is a scientist who studies the remnants of ancient life by examining fossilized remains, such as bones or shells. Sometimes, paleontologists only have a few bones to help in determining the type of animal from which the bones came. They also may try to determine what the animal ate, where it lived, and how it may have died. In the rare instance when the complete skeleton of a new type of animal is found, paleontologists attempt to piece together the bones of the animal. This is similar to putting together a puzzle without having a picture to look at.

MATERIALS

Mystery Animal Bones worksheet (page 41)	construction paper
scissors	glue

PROCEDURE:

1. Carefully cut out each bone from the Mystery Animal Bones worksheet.

2. Many species have bones that are similar in appearance and function. Use a science book, an encyclopedia, or the Internet to find a labeled diagram of a human skeleton. Use this to guide you as you piece together the mystery animal bones.

3. Once you have pieced the skeleton together, have your teacher check it. Then, glue the completed skeleton to a piece of construction paper.

CONCLUSIONS:

1. What type of animal did you piece together? _____

2. How is this activity similar to the work of a real paleontologist? How is it different?

   _____

   _____

3. Why is it important for paleontologists to be experts in both anatomy and geology?

   _____

   _____

4. Sometimes several skeletons are found buried together in the same location. Why would this make a paleontologist's job more challenging?

   _____

   _____

MYSTERY ANIMAL BONES

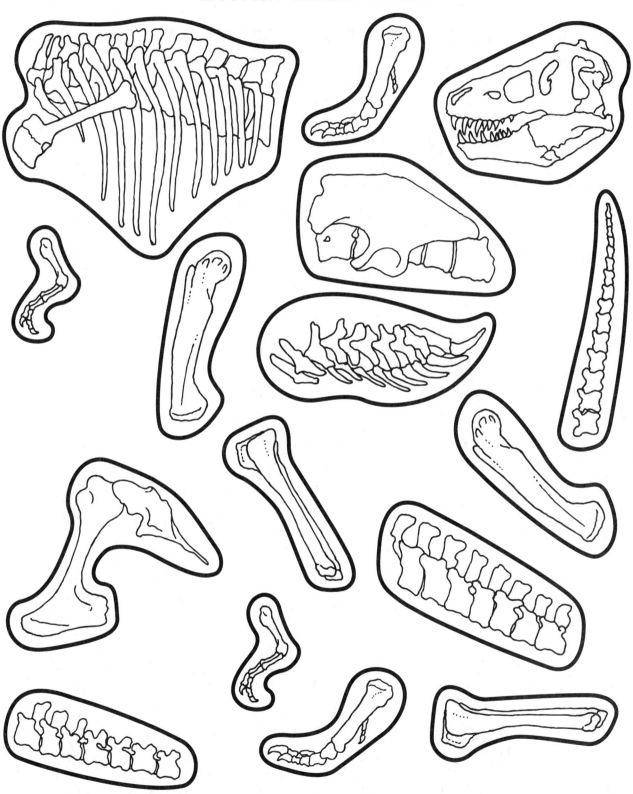

Earth's Shifting Surface

DIRECTIONS: Find the plate tectonics vocabulary words in the word search puzzle below. Words can be found across, down, and diagonally. Then, on a separate piece of paper, write sentences for five of the words.

WORD BANK

asthenosphere	crust	mantle	subduction
continental drift	divergent	outer core	transform
convergent	inner core	plates	Wegener
core	lithosphere	seafloor spreading	

```
O  H  N  C  Z  L  W  Z  L  F  T  H  S  G  U  Q  G  Z  N  T
U  I  H  Y  G  F  W  J  C  L  V  X  E  E  O  Y  X  E  T  D
T  I  Q  T  X  G  Q  A  E  I  L  P  A  P  C  O  D  X  S  V
E  L  L  J  M  B  N  R  C  T  A  W  F  A  W  U  T  Q  U  Z
R  B  D  C  T  W  O  G  R  H  E  F  L  O  P  D  Z  T  B  T
C  W  Z  O  R  C  R  J  D  O  Q  D  O  A  C  D  T  L  D  K
O  V  W  N  F  V  F  S  R  S  N  H  O  E  I  P  U  L  U  W
R  R  A  T  C  Q  F  H  Y  P  F  E  R  P  N  T  I  C  C  N
E  W  S  I  V  H  O  A  M  H  G  Z  S  X  L  R  D  O  T  G
U  K  T  N  E  G  J  O  P  E  R  X  P  G  H  A  J  N  I  S
N  J  H  E  H  I  T  V  O  R  D  Q  R  K  I  T  T  V  O  D
I  A  E  N  M  A  N  T  L  E  W  L  E  Q  E  R  H  E  N  I
C  J  N  T  E  R  W  N  E  X  H  X  A  Y  Z  A  X  R  S  V
D  N  O  A  G  N  E  R  E  X  T  B  D  H  M  N  B  G  B  E
V  I  S  L  C  M  G  Y  M  R  W  M  I  R  C  S  I  E  F  R
X  L  P  D  R  I  E  J  Q  Y  C  G  N  B  X  F  V  N  A  G
G  W  H  R  U  B  N  N  J  D  B  O  G  C  C  O  M  T  L  E
M  L  E  I  S  G  E  R  H  W  B  C  R  V  J  R  I  S  C  N
A  D  R  F  T  I  R  F  B  C  A  L  M  E  C  M  X  P  Y  T
F  A  E  T  X  U  V  Z  K  T  U  E  Y  C  Q  X  S  Z  L  A
```

Earth's Shifting Surface

DIRECTIONS: Complete the crossword puzzle.

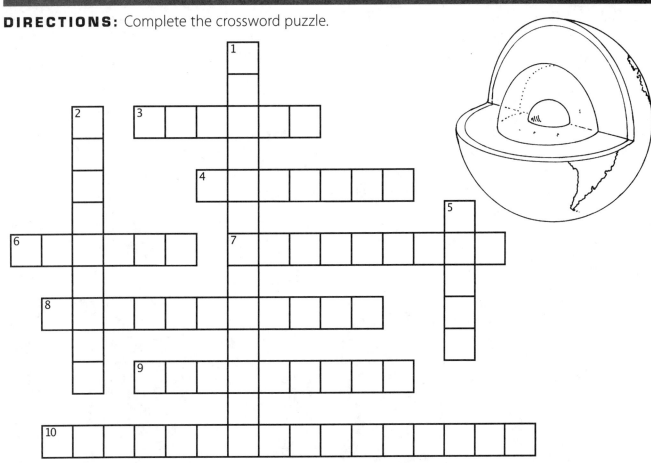

ACROSS

3. thickest layer of Earth; located between the crust and core

4. scientist who proposed the theory of continental drift

6. Earth's crust is divided into many different tectonic _____.

7. layer of liquid iron and nickel that lies under the mantle and surrounds the inner core

8. rigid layer of Earth consisting of the crust and upper part of the mantle

9. dense center of Earth; made of solid iron and nickel

10. theory that the continents are slowing moving apart from each other

DOWN

1. pieces of lithosphere move slowly over this soft layer of the mantle

2. Seafloor _____ is the process by which new crust is created when the seafloor moves apart and magma rises up.

5. thinnest, outermost layer of Earth; ranges from 5 to 100 km thick

The Puzzle of Pangaea

Millions of years ago, Earth was a very different place. Since that time, climates have changed and different species have emerged, evolved, and become extinct. Landforms also have changed dramatically. In 1912, a scientist named **Alfred Wegener** introduced his **theory of continental drift**. Wegener had noticed the continents could be pieced together like a rough puzzle. The continents fit together to form one large continent that Wegener called **Pangaea**.

Earth's crust is broken into many pieces. These pieces are called **plates**. There are 12 main plates on the earth's surface, which slide very slowly on the mantle's upper layer. Over time, the plates have slowly changed positions and have moved the continents into their present-day locations. The plates are still moving very slowly, at a rate of one to two centimeters per year!

Cut out the seven present-day continents below. Then, try to piece them together to form the continent of Pangaea. Be aware that the continents will not fit together exactly. Over millions of years, the levels of the oceans have varied. The oceans have eroded and changed the coastlines of the continents.

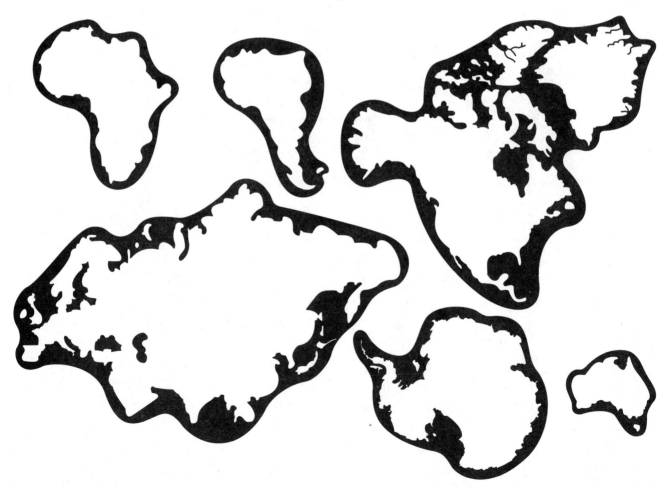

A Controversial Idea

CREATIVE WRITING

In 1912, Alfred Wegener proposed his ideas on **continental drift**. According to his hypothesis, the continents have not always been in their current locations. Rather, over millions of years, they have slowly moved into their present-day positions.

Many other scientists did not accept Wegener's ideas at the time; they felt he could not provide enough evidence in favor of them. Since then, scientists have discovered more evidence to prove the theory of continental drift.

DIRECTIONS: Pretend that you are Alfred Wegener and you are living now. You have your original evidence for continental drift, plus all of the newer evidence discovered by other scientists that supports your ideas. Write a speech that outlines the evidence and attempt to convince today's scientists that your ideas are correct.

_____

_____

_____

_____

_____

_____

_____

_____

_____

_____

_____

_____

_____

_____

_____

_____

Know Your Boundaries

DIRECTIONS: Write each letter in the correct blank to match each vocabulary term with its definition. Then, use the same terms to label the diagrams below. Some diagrams can be labeled with more than one term.

1. ____ transform

2. ____ seafloor spreading

3. ____ continental collision

4. ____ convergent

5. ____ rift valley

6. ____ divergent

7. ____ subduction

a. When two tectonic plates push into each other, the place the two plates meet is called a _____ boundary.

b. When two tectonic plates move away from each other, the boundary between them is called a _____ boundary.

c. When two tectonic plates slide past each other horizontally, the boundary between them is called a _____ boundary.

d. New crust is created when the seafloor moves apart. New magma continuously rises up to fill in the space. This process is called _____.

e. A _____ zone is where a continental plate and an oceanic plate collide, forcing the oceanic plate under the less dense continental plate.

f. A _____ forms at the place where two continental plates pull apart.

g. A _____ occurs when two continental plates collide, pushing the continental crust up to form mountains.

8. _____

9. _____

10. _____

11. _____

Name: _____   Date: _____

Inside the Earth

DIAGRAM LABELING / FILL IN THE BLANKS

DIRECTIONS: Write each term from the word bank in the correct blank to label the diagram of Earth's interior. Then, write each term next to its correct description below.

WORD BANK

lithosphere	mantle	outer core
asthenosphere	inner core	crust

1. _____

2. _____

3. _____

4. _____

5. _____

6. _____

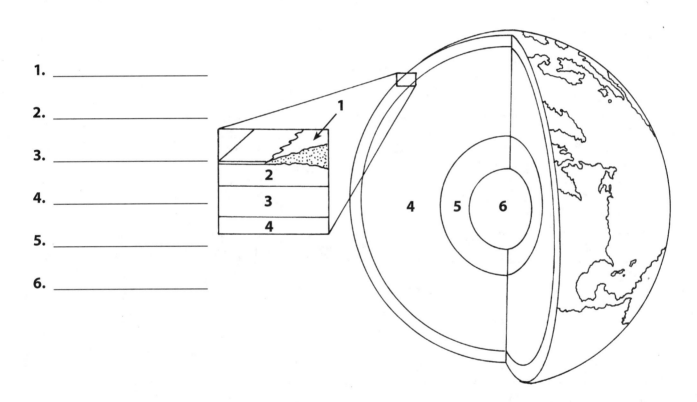

7. _____ layer of molten iron and nickel that surrounds the inner core

8. _____ thinnest, outermost layer of Earth; ranges from 5 to 100 km thick

9. _____ layer of hot, solid material between the crust and Earth's core

10. _____ rigid layer consisting of the crust and uppermost part of the mantle

11. _____ dense sphere of solid iron and nickel at the center of Earth

12. _____ soft layer of the mantle on which pieces of lithosphere slowly float

PLATE TECTONICS

A Current Event

INQUIRY INVESTIGATION

A pot of water on a stove will experience rising and sinking water currents due to the unequal heating of the pot. When the stove is on, hot, less dense water rises. As the hot water reaches the surface, it cools and sinks to the bottom of the pot. This process is similar to what happens to molten rocks in Earth's mantle. These movements of a material are called **convection currents**.

MATERIALS

9" x 13" (32 x 23 x 5 cm) clear glass baking dish	portable stove top	food coloring
	water	oven mitts

PROCEDURE:

1. Fill the baking dish half full with water.

2. Carefully place the dish on the portable stove top. Turn the stove on to a low temperature. The dish will become hot quickly. If you need to adjust the position of the baking dish, wear oven mitts.

3. Add a few drops of food coloring to the water in the center of the dish. Observe the movement of the water in the dish. Draw a diagram of what happens in the chart below.

4. Try adding food coloring to different locations in the dish. Draw a diagram of what happens in the chart.

Center	Left Side	Right Side

CONCLUSIONS:

1. Describe the convection currents that occurred in the heated baking dish of water.

    _____

    _____

2. In your own words, describe what caused the convection currents that occurred in the dish.

    _____

    _____

Quaking, Shaking Earth

WORD SEARCH

DIRECTIONS: Find the earthquake vocabulary words in the word search puzzle below. Words can be found across, down, and diagonally. Then, on a separate piece of paper, write sentences for five of the words.

WORD BANK

epicenter	magnitude	secondary wave	seismic waves	reverse
fault	primary wave	seismograph	seismology	strike-slip
focus	Richter scale	surface wave	normal	

```
D  L  K  Y  O  U  W  R  E  V  E  R  S  E  P  O  F  B  P  K
X  L  R  R  C  Y  C  G  P  B  E  X  R  H  Z  P  D  V  Q  C
E  Q  H  V  J  Z  Q  V  Q  C  C  P  H  D  J  A  P  M  O  R
M  G  M  F  J  H  X  I  D  B  S  A  I  L  R  Q  Y  O  D  I
S  C  E  A  T  C  B  M  X  O  F  B  R  C  T  N  W  C  C  S
W  D  W  J  G  O  K  A  F  K  L  O  I  V  E  M  T  X  J  S
N  W  I  Z  S  N  Q  N  B  Y  W  M  C  G  X  N  P  L  C  T
J  S  B  W  E  D  I  S  F  O  T  S  H  U  L  S  T  S  V  R
S  F  K  T  C  T  Q  T  Z  F  V  E  T  Z  S  E  R  E  P  I
L  U  X  X  O  S  V  Z  U  Q  D  I  E  T  U  I  C  I  R  K
S  H  R  K  N  J  B  U  V  D  U  S  R  D  P  S  L  S  I  E
F  I  T  F  D  O  N  Z  G  O  E  M  S  F  R  M  Q  M  M  S
J  X  J  J  A  E  R  K  T  K  B  O  C  F  A  I  F  O  A  L
R  B  U  Q  R  C  K  M  L  D  N  L  A  A  F  C  S  G  R  I
P  F  D  D  Y  Q  E  Y  A  J  G  O  L  U  W  W  R  R  Y  P
B  J  C  I  W  C  N  W  Q  L  P  G  E  L  A  A  V  A  W  C
U  L  X  K  A  F  Y  S  A  H  N  Y  C  T  W  V  L  P  A  U
S  P  Q  T  V  J  W  X  K  V  A  I  I  V  Y  E  W  H  V  L
C  L  F  P  E  C  A  B  G  W  E  A  Y  Z  F  S  Q  Q  E  Y
```

Name: _____   Date: _____

Quaking, Shaking Earth

CROSSWORD PUZZLE

DIRECTIONS: Complete the crossword puzzle.

ACROSS

3. the study of earthquakes and seismic waves that move through and around Earth

5. the waves that arrive after primary waves; they move the ground back and forth

6. an instrument that records seismic waves

7. measure of released energy of an earthquake

8. point on Earth's crust directly above the focus of an earthquake

DOWN

1. break in Earth's crust where pieces of the crust move relative to each other

2. the fastest waves that compress and expand the ground like an accordion

3. waves that can make the ground roll like ocean waves; they usually cause the most damage during an earthquake

4. point inside Earth where rock that is under stress breaks causing an earthquake

5. energy waves that are vibrations traveling through Earth

Earthquake Travel Times

When an earthquake occurs, **seismic waves** are produced that move outward in all directions from the focus. The **focus** is the point in the earth where energy is released. There are two basic types of seismic waves. **Primary waves**, or P waves, travel faster and are the first waves to arrive at distant seismic observation stations. **Secondary waves**, or S waves, travel slower and arrive at observation stations after the P waves. Although P and S waves start at the same time, they get farther apart as they travel away from the earthquake.

DIRECTIONS: Use the graph of travel times for P and S waves to answer the questions below.

1. How long does it take a P wave to travel 2,000 km?

   _____

2. How long does it take an S wave to travel 3,000 km?

   _____

3. How far does a P wave travel in four minutes?

   _____

4. How far does an S wave travel in four minutes?

   _____

5. If both waves travel for six minutes, which wave travels farther?

   _____

6. What happens to the time difference between P and S waves as the distance the waves travel increases?

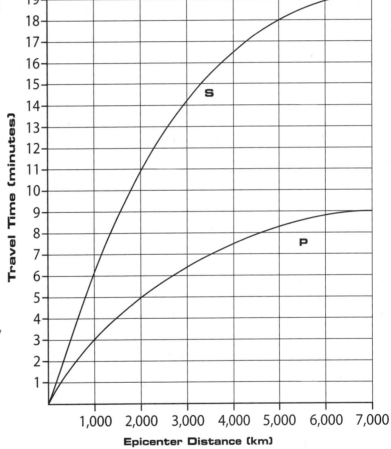

_____

7. About how far away is the epicenter from a seismograph station that recorded a five-minute difference between P wave and S wave arrival times?

_____

Earthquake Locations

DIRECTIONS: The map on page 53 shows the major tectonic plates on Earth. Use an atlas to find the location of each earthquake epicenter listed below. Mark each city or area on the map with a small dot. Then, answer the questions below.

Past Earthquake Epicenters		
Shaanxi, China	San Francisco, CA, United States	Loma Prieta, CA, United States
Calcutta, India	Tokyo, Japan	Kobe, Japan
Lisbon, Portugal	Concepción, Chile	Northridge, CA, United States
New Madrid, MO, United States	Tangshan, China	Maharashtra, India
Charleston, SC, United States	Mexico City, Mexico	Luzon, Philippines

1. Are any of these earthquake epicenters found along plate boundaries? If so, why do you think earthquakes have occurred there in the past?

   _____

   _____

   _____

2. In which of the above locations would an earthquake be most likely to occur in the future? Why?

   _____

   _____

   _____

3. Where do you think people are relatively safe from earthquakes? Why?

   _____

   _____

   _____

4. Why is a map showing locations of past earthquakes useful to scientists?

   _____

   _____

   _____

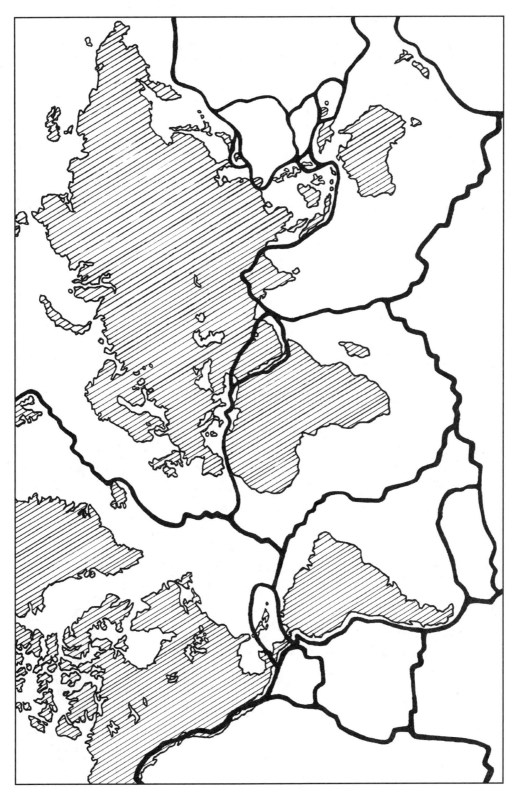

Whose "Fault" Is It?

A **fault** is a break in Earth's crust where pieces of the crust slip past each other. The rocks on both sides of the fault can move up, down, or sideways. There are three main kinds of faults: **normal**, **reverse**, and **strike-slip**. Label each diagram below by writing the type of fault it represents in the correct blank. Then, write the type of fault below its definition at the bottom of the page.

1. This type of fault is caused by tension forces.

   _____

2. This type of fault is caused by shear forces.

   _____

3. This type of fault is caused by compression forces.

   _____

4. Rocks on either side of the fault move past each other without moving up or down. The San Andreas Fault is an example of this type of fault.

   _____

5. Rocks on one side of the fault move down in relation to rocks on the opposite side of the fault. The Teton Range in Grand Teton National Park was produced by this type of fault.

   _____

6. Rocks on one side of the fault are forced up and over the rocks on the opposite side of the fault. This type of fault produced the Appalachian Mountains range in the eastern United States.

   _____

Quaking Elsewhere!

Earthquakes are vibrations that are produced by the movement of pieces of Earth's crust. While we usually only think of quakes that occur here on Earth, other objects in our solar system experience different types of quakes.

DIRECTIONS: Use science books, encyclopedias, or the Internet to research quakes that occur on the sun, moon, and Mars. Then, compare and contrast these quakes with earthquakes. If you need additional space, continue your descriptions on a separate piece of paper.

Sunquakes: _____

_____

_____

Moonquakes: _____

_____

_____

Marsquakes: _____

_____

_____

Type of Quakes	How are they similar to earthquakes?	How are they different from earthquakes?
Sunquakes		
Moonquakes		
Marsquakes		

Name: _____ Date: _____

Shakedown!

Engineers who design buildings for earthquake-prone areas must keep the possibility of earthquakes in mind. People can be injured by the total or partial collapse of a building. They can also be injured by pieces, such as broken glass, falling from structures. It would be very expensive and difficult to create a building that is "earthquake proof." Instead, engineers try to create **earthquake-resistant** buildings. These are buildings that may suffer damage but will keep the people inside and around the outside of the building safe. In this activity, you will become an engineer who designs an earthquake-resistant skyscraper.

MATERIALS

building blocks	craft sticks	toothpicks	any additional teacher-approved materials
dictionary	rubber bands	meterstick	

PROCEDURE:

1. Stack 8–10 blocks on top of each other on your desk to create a skyscraper. Draw a picture of the skyscraper in the chart below.

2. Hold the dictionary one meter above your desk. Drop it onto the desk next to the skyscraper. Record your observations in the chart.

Drawing of Skyscraper	Effect of Earthquake

3. Use the blocks and the other building materials to create a skyscraper that can resist the shaking caused by the dictionary being dropped onto the desk. You may use some or all of the materials. Draw a picture of the skyscraper in the chart below.

4. Repeat step 2 with the improved skyscraper design. Record your observations in the chart.

Drawing of Skyscraper	Effect of Earthquake
	_____
	_____
	_____
	_____
	_____
	_____

CONCLUSIONS:

1. What caused the first skyscraper to topple when the book was dropped?

_____

_____

2. Describe how you altered the second skyscraper to make it earthquake resistant.

_____

_____

3. Use science books, encyclopedias, or the Internet to conduct research on ways engineers design earthquake-resistant buildings. What additional changes could you make to your skyscraper?

_____

_____

_____

Earth's Cooling Vents

W O R D   S E A R C H

DIRECTIONS: Find the volcano vocabulary words in the word search puzzle below. Words can be found across, down, and diagonally. Then, on a separate piece of paper, write sentences for five of the words.

WORD BANK

crater	lava	magma	lapilli	pahoehoe
composite	hot spot	cinder cone	volcanic bombs	volcanic blocks
pyroclastic	shield	rift	pillow lava	
volcano	caldera	volcanic ash	aa	

```
I  Y  U  U  W  R  S  M  N  U  F  H  D  O  M  L  O  F  K  D
I  W  B  O  C  L  M  Q  M  R  S  A  J  R  P  C  L  S  V  Y
V  V  D  Q  F  M  U  B  J  A  I  H  J  S  X  G  A  R  W  X
U  A  O  I  J  G  M  E  C  P  J  F  O  R  D  A  V  Z  B  V
F  Z  Z  L  D  N  P  I  F  I  C  M  T  T  F  A  A  U  C  C
R  O  V  R  C  T  N  Y  C  L  I  B  A  D  S  Z  M  X  X  S
G  A  X  X  S  A  M  R  O  L  N  B  S  G  F  P  N  S  H  V
H  M  L  C  C  Q  N  Q  A  O  D  P  Z  A  M  Z  O  Y  P  O
C  L  C  L  R  A  B  O  P  W  E  Q  H  A  Q  A  G  T  D  L
K  B  O  O  P  A  Y  B  N  L  R  P  N  U  I  G  U  L  D  C
P  V  D  D  M  D  T  E  S  A  C  M  H  Y  V  R  E  S  M  A
A  T  X  B  K  P  W  E  N  V  O  V  R  X  M  I  H  H  N  N
H  I  F  T  A  V  O  F  R  A  N  E  R  P  H  J  R  J  J  I
O  B  A  Z  L  S  F  S  R  K  E  X  U  S  X  D  H  N  S  C
E  B  E  F  A  C  Q  M  I  G  H  P  Q  K  M  E  P  Y  F  B
H  V  U  I  P  E  N  Y  A  T  P  X  C  X  Z  Z  P  P  U  L
O  R  Z  X  V  I  C  A  L  D  E  R  A  C  B  V  Z  S  A  O
E  L  A  P  I  L  L  I  D  N  V  U  T  Y  O  O  B  H  N  C
Q  D  F  V  O  L  C  A  N  I  C  B  O  M  B  S  Q  A  Z  K
X  P  Y  R  O  C  L  A  S  T  I  C  L  P  P  V  I  W  A  S
```

Name: _____ Date: _____

Earth's Cooling Vents

C R O S S W O R D   P U Z Z L E

DIRECTIONS: Complete the crossword puzzle.

ACROSS

5. A _____ volcano is a broad mountain that forms when explosive eruptions of ash, cinder, and bombs alternate with quiet lava flows.

8. liquid magma that has reached Earth's surface

9. an unusually hot area deep in Earth's mantle that melts the crust above it and forms a volcano

10. central, funnel-shaped vent at the top of a volcano

DOWN

1. A _____ volcano forms from quiet eruptions of lava that spread out in flat layers to create wide, gentle slopes.

2. _____ flows are violent explosions of ash, cinders, bombs, and gases from a volcano.

3. an opening in Earth's crust where magma, comes to the surface; often forms a mountain

4. _____ volcanoes occur where two tectonic plates move apart and magma rises up to create new crust.

5. A _____ volcano is a steep-sided, cone-shaped hill that is created by the eruption of volcanic ash, cinders, and bombs around the volcano's opening.

6. molten rock under Earth's crust in the mantle

7. the large, circular depression at the top of a volcano that forms when the roof of the magma chamber collapses

Flowing Eruptions

MYSTERY WORD

DIRECTIONS: Write each volcano term in the correct blank to match the term with its definition below. Circle the named letter in each answer. Then, unscramble the circled letters to reveal the mystery word.

WORD BANK

pillow	volcanic ash	volcanic bombs	volcanic blocks
lapilli	pahoehoe	aa	

1. _____ Hawaiian term for lava that flows slowly, with rounded folds

2. _____ Hawaiian term for lava that has a rough surface made of broken lava blocks (first letter)

3. _____ type of lava that erupts underwater and takes the form of round lumps (sixth letter)

4. _____ These pieces of lava fragments are ejected from a volcano while they are still molten (liquid). The fragments form rounded shapes during their travel through the air. (seventh letter)

5. _____ These solid rock fragments are ejected from a volcano during an explosive eruption. They commonly are formed from solid pieces of old lava flows that were part of the volcano's cone. (fifth letter)

6. _____ small pebble-sized rock fragments ejected from a volcano during an explosive eruption (fourth letter)

7. _____ This is created during explosive eruptions by the shattering of solid rocks and the violent separation of magma into tiny pieces about the size of a pinhead. It rises quickly to form a towering eruption column directly above the volcano. (eleventh letter)

MYSTERY WORD: This U.S. state was formed entirely by volcanic activity.

____ ____ ____ ____ ____ ____

Movement Inside the Earth

D I A G R A M   L A B E L I N G / F I L L   I N   T H E   B L A N K S

Most people think of volcanic activity as something that occurs on Earth's surface. However, a lot of activity occurs below ground and never reaches the surface. This type of below-ground activity results in rock formations that are sometimes exposed over time by erosion.

DIRECTIONS: Study the diagram of underground volcanic features. Write each type of rock formation from the word bank in the correct blank to label the diagram. Then, write each word next to its correct definition below.

W O R D   B A N K

| batholith | volcanic neck | dike | sill |

1. _____   **3.** _____

2. _____   **4.** _____

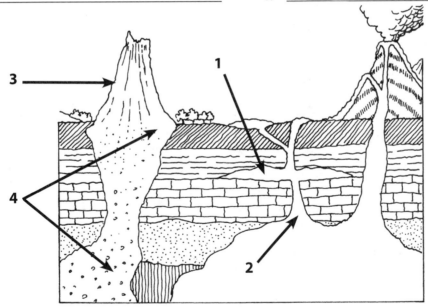

5. _____   solid core of a volcano left behind after the volcano's cone has eroded away

6. _____   formed when magma is squeezed into a horizontal crack between layers of rock and hardens underground

7. _____   formed when magma is squeezed into a vertical crack that cuts across rock layers and hardens underground

8. _____   formed when a magma chamber cools slowly and hardens underground

VOLCANOES

Otherworldly Volcanoes

C R E A T I V E   W R I T I N G

Earth is not the only place in the solar system with volcanoes on its surface. Mars, Venus, and Europa (a moon of Jupiter) are believed to have once had active volcanoes. On another of Jupiter's moons, Io, volcanoes are still active! In the mid-1990s, the space probe *Galileo* photographed an eruption occurring on Io. Scientists also think that ice-covered Europa may have ancient volcanoes that erupted water. Mars has many ancient volcanoes, including the largest in the entire solar system, Olympus Mons. The *Magellan* spacecraft used radar to reveal ancient volcanoes on Venus.

DIRECTIONS: Use science books, encyclopedias, or the Internet to research volcanoes found on Io, Europa, Venus, or Mars. Then, write a persuasive letter to NASA outlining the reasons you would like to send a mission to this planet or moon.

_____

_____

_____

_____

_____

_____

_____

_____

_____

_____

_____

_____

_____

_____

_____

_____

_____

_____

VOLCANOES

Lava in the Lab—Part I

INQUIRY INVESTIGATION

Many different factors affect how lava flows during a volcanic eruption. In this investigation, you will examine how temperature affects the rate that lava flows.

MATERIALS

corn syrup	thermometer	paper plate
2 large glass beakers	teaspoon	meterstick
5 small glass beakers	beaker tongs	water
hot plate	stopwatch	small ice cubes or crushed ice

PROCEDURE:

1. Pour 25 mL of corn syrup into each of the five small glass beakers.

2. Place the first small beaker of corn syrup into one of the large beakers. Carefully pack ice around the outside of the small beaker.

3. Set aside the second small beaker of corn syrup. This syrup will be tested at room temperature.

4. Fill the other large glass beaker half full with water. Carefully place the third small beaker of corn syrup inside it. Place a thermometer into the syrup in the small beaker and place both beakers on the hot plate. Heat the corn syrup to 25°C. Caution: Be careful when handling hot liquids and using heating equipment, such as hot plates.

5. Use the beaker tongs to remove the beakers from the hot plate.

6. Remove one teaspoon of the heated corn syrup from the beaker and hold it 30 cm above the paper plate. Turn the spoon on its side. Use the stopwatch to time how long it takes for a drop of syrup to hit the plate. Record the time in the data table on page 64.

7. Choose two additional temperatures to which you will heat the two remaining beakers of corn syrup. (Do not heat the syrup over 50°C.) Write these temperatures in the data table on page 64. Then, repeat steps 4–6 with these two beakers of syrup.

8. Record the temperatures of the samples of corn syrup in ice and at room temperature. Then, repeat step 6 with each one.

Trial	Syrup Temperature (°C)	Time Taken to Fall 30 cm (seconds)
Heated Sample 1	25°C	
Heated Sample 2		
Heated Sample 3		
Syrup in Ice		
Syrup at Room Temperature		

CONCLUSIONS:

1. At which temperature did the drop of syrup take the longest time to fall? Why do you think this happened?

   _____

   _____

   _____

2. Which sample took the shortest amount of time to fall? Why do you think this happened?

   _____

   _____

   _____

3. How can you relate this experiment to lava flows and types of volcanoes?

   _____

   _____

Name: _____ Date: _____

Lava in the Lab—Part 2

INQUIRY INVESTIGATION

Many factors besides temperature affect the rate that lava flows during a volcanic eruption. For example, the amount and types of minerals, the amount of fluid, and the amount of air in lava all change the way it flows and the type of volcano it forms.

DIRECTIONS: Design an experiment to test one of the variables listed above. Think about how each one could be tested in the lab using everyday materials. Since you already tested temperature in Lava in the Lab—Part 1, choose a different variable this time.

List the variable being tested and the materials you will need below. Use the table to display your data. On a separate piece of paper, write a numbered procedure. After you have completed the investigation, write a conclusion paragraph that explains what you learned and how the experiment relates to lava flows.

VARIABLE BEING TESTED: _____

MATERIALS

- _____
- _____
- _____
- _____

- _____
- _____
- _____
- _____

DATA TABLE:

A Cycle of Water

DIAGRAM LABELING/FILL IN THE BLANKS

The amount of water on Earth today is exactly the same amount that was here millions of years ago. A special process called the **water cycle** is continuously moving water from Earth's surface into the atmosphere and then back again.

DIRECTIONS: Study the diagram of the water cycle. Write each water cycle term from the word bank in the correct blank to label the diagram. Then, write each term next to its correct definition below.

WORD BANK

runoff	precipitation	evaporation
transpiration	condensation	infiltration

1. _____

2. _____

3. _____

4. _____

5. _____

6. _____

7. _____ water in the form of rain, snow, sleet, or hail that falls from clouds onto Earth's surface

8. _____ the process by which clouds form as water vapor cools and changes into liquid water droplets

9. _____ how water soaks down into the ground

10. _____ water that flows across land and into streams, rivers, or oceans

11. _____ the process by which water on Earth's surface changes from liquid to water vapor

12. _____ evaporation of water into the atmosphere from the leaves and stems of plants

Rivers and Streams

DIRECTIONS: Find the river and stream vocabulary words in the word search puzzle below. Words can be found across, down, and diagonally. Then, on a separate piece of paper, write sentences for five of the words.

WORD BANK

drainage basin	tributary	delta	water cycle	erosion
meander	channel	load	deposition	alluvial fan
divide	runoff	floodplain	discharge	

```
U  N  F  K  Z  C  Y  N  P  O  D  I  S  C  H  A  R  G  E  R
O  X  A  I  Q  K  X  U  T  F  Z  I  S  O  I  H  E  O  L  L
D  N  R  N  R  Z  T  L  S  K  X  M  N  L  F  A  W  R  I  J
I  B  C  E  K  N  F  R  O  G  Y  L  I  G  L  I  P  D  E  C
V  K  H  V  K  D  D  F  I  A  Z  X  V  H  F  D  X  R  F  V
I  M  P  K  S  F  E  D  V  B  D  P  G  T  T  A  D  A  W  R
D  U  Z  L  I  O  H  E  D  R  U  D  X  R  C  B  E  I  W  Y
E  I  M  V  A  Y  N  L  J  D  T  T  W  U  A  R  P  N  J  I
G  C  C  M  R  L  Z  T  N  S  E  M  A  X  E  U  O  A  N  X
A  F  X  H  Z  U  Q  A  J  L  R  O  T  R  D  V  S  G  Q  G
O  R  X  V  A  Z  N  F  M  T  O  O  E  Q  Y  Z  I  E  M  B
C  G  W  G  X  N  O  O  T  E  S  S  R  C  K  Z  T  B  E  Q
S  G  O  G  M  I  N  L  F  V  I  E  C  P  E  S  I  A  A  S
D  M  K  W  C  M  V  E  A  F  O  W  Y  X  D  Y  O  S  N  Q
H  T  Z  D  W  L  V  C  L  O  N  I  C  N  Z  Y  N  I  D  L
V  D  M  E  Z  S  M  J  O  S  L  N  L  B  M  K  M  N  E  O
X  F  L  O  O  D  P  L  A  I  N  Y  E  K  E  P  K  D  R  S
D  N  D  V  K  D  X  D  G  Q  A  V  R  F  R  C  N  W  L
N  A  A  V  A  L  L  U  V  I  A  L  F  A  N  J  C  E  T  R
U  E  W  X  K  V  W  C  Q  U  L  W  M  P  F  J  W  Q  V  N
```

FRESHWATER

Rivers and Streams

CROSSWORD PUZZLE

DIRECTIONS: Complete the crossword puzzle.

ACROSS

1. the land area from which rivers and tributaries collect their water

2. area that separates drainage basins

3. the continuous movement of water from Earth's surface to the atmosphere and back again

6. flat, wide area of land along a river that floods when the river overflows

7. small stream or river that flows into a larger stream or river

9. the path followed by a stream

11. loop-like curve in a river or stream

12. particles carried by a stream or river

DOWN

1. amount of water carried by a stream or river

2. process that occurs when water slows down and particles of rock and sand are laid down in new locations

4. fan-shaped deposits of rock and soil

5. movement of rock and soil through weathering

8. rainwater that has not evaporated or soaked into the ground and flows over Earth's surface into rivers, streams, and oceans

10. a landform created when a river reaches a large body of water (such as an ocean) and deposits sediments

The Groundwater Shuffle

M A G I C   N U M B E R

DIRECTIONS: Write each letter in the correct blank to match each vocabulary term with its definition. Then, copy the number of each answer into the box below with the matching letter. When you add the numbers down, across, and diagonally, the sums should be the same.

2. _____ groundwater

4. _____ water table

6. _____ aquifer

8. _____ porosity

10. _____ permeability

12. _____ artesian spring

14. _____ recharge zone

16. _____ zone of aeration

18. _____ zone of saturation

a. the upper level of the ground where open spaces in the rock and soil are filled with water

b. layer of rocks and soil below the water table; usually filled with water

c. the amount of open space between rocks

d. the point on Earth's surface where water enters an aquifer

e. the ability of water to pass through a rock

f. a layer of rock that stores water while allowing it to move freely underground

g. water flows from this when the water table reaches Earth's surface

h. water located under Earth's surface

i. layer of rocks and soil above the water table that are usually not filled with water

a.	b.	c.
d.	e.	f.
g.	h.	i.

MAGIC NUMBER = _____

Stream Stages

Streams and rivers come in many shapes, sizes, and forms. Some are wide and slow moving, while others are narrow and fast. Although scientists can accurately describe a stream's current stage of development, they often have a difficult time determining its age.

Young streams flow swiftly, often over rapids and waterfalls. They are usually narrow with steep sides.

Mature streams are formed when many of the rocks that cause rapids are eroded away. As streams mature, they reach level ground, the discharge slows, and they begin to form meanders.

Old streams are very wide with strong meanders and flow smoothly and slowly through a flat area of land. They are found in floodplains and often deposit sediment along their banks or into deltas.

DIRECTIONS: Look at each stream diagram below. Label each stream as young, mature, or old. Then, describe the reasons you think the stream is in that stage.

1. Type of stream:

_____

Reasons:

_____

_____

2. Type of stream:

_____

Reasons:

_____

_____

3. Type of stream:

_____

Reasons:

_____

_____

FRESHWATER

Speeding Streams and Rivers—Part 1

MATH SKILLS

Scientists who study streams and rivers classify them by measuring the slope of the ground that they flow over. Streams and rivers that flow over steep ground flow quickly, while streams and rivers that flow over flatter ground are slower moving. Scientists have a method of determining the speed of the water in a stream or river by using the following simple math equation.

speed = distance/time

To figure out the speed of the water in a stream or river, you need to find the distance that the water travels over a set amount of time. First, look at the example. Then, try a few of your own below.

EXAMPLE

If the water in the river travels 10 meters in 5 seconds, what is the speed of the river?

distance: 10 meters   **time:** 5 seconds   **speed =** ?

speed = 10 m/5 sec. = 2 m/sec.

1. If the water in the river travels 20 meters in 5 seconds, what is the speed of the river?

    distance: _____

    time: _____

    speed: _____

2. If the water in the river travels 10 meters in 20 seconds, what is the speed of the river?

    distance: _____

    time: _____

    speed: _____

3. If the water in the river travels 100 meters in 10 seconds, what is the speed of the river?

    distance: _____

    time: _____

    speed: _____

4. If the speed of the river is 2 m/sec., how long did the water take to travel 20 meters?

    distance: _____

    time: _____

    speed: _____

5. Which of these rivers (1–4) is most likely a young river? Explain your answer.

    _____

    _____

    _____

6. Which of these rivers (1–4) is most likely an old river? Explain your answer.

    _____

    _____

    _____

Speeding Streams and Rivers—Part 2

In this activity, you and two partners will determine the speed of a local stream.

MATERIALS

| 3 oranges | stopwatch | meterstick |

PROCEDURE:

1. Use the meterstick to measure a distance of 10 meters along the bank of a stream or river. One student should stand at the beginning of the 10 meters, and another should stand downstream at the end of the 10 meters with a stopwatch.

2. Stand a few meters upstream from the first student and toss an orange in the water. When the orange gets to the first student, she should yell "Go!"

3. The student with the stopwatch should start timing. The stopwatch should be stopped when the orange reaches the end of the 10 meters where he is standing.

4. Repeat steps 2 and 3 two additional times. Record the data in the table below.

5. Using the equation, **speed = distance/time**, find the speed of the stream for each trial.

6. Find the average speed of the stream. Record it in the table.

Distance (m)	Time (sec.)	Speed (m/sec.)
10 meters		
10 meters		
10 meters		
Average Speed =		

CONCLUSIONS: Answer the following questions on a separate piece of paper.

1. Why do you think the orange should be tossed in a little ahead of the 10-meter starting point?

2. Why do you think the experiment was done three times, rather than just once?

3. Based on your calculations and observations of the stream, do you think it is young, mature, or old? Explain.

4. What are some sources of error in this experiment?

The Life and Times of a Water Droplet

C R E A T I V E   W R I T I N G

Fill a glass with water. Look closely at the water in the glass. Can you guess how old it is? The water in the glass may have fallen as rain last week, but the **water cycle** has been moving this water around Earth for millions of years. When an apatosaurus took a drink from a lake, your glass of water may have been a part of that lake. When Columbus sailed across the Atlantic Ocean, that same water may have rushed by one of his three ships. Imagine the story one drop of water could tell—it would be an amazing tale!

DIRECTIONS: Pretend that you are a drop of water in a puddle on your street. How did you get into the puddle? Where are you going next? Use pages 66–72 as references as you write a short story that describes your journey through the water cycle. If you need additional space, continue your writing on a separate piece of paper.

_____

_____

_____

_____

_____

_____

_____

_____

_____

_____

_____

_____

The Living Ocean

W O R D   S E A R C H

DIRECTIONS: Find the ocean vocabulary words in the word search puzzle below. Words can be found across, down, and diagonally. Then, on a separate piece of paper, write sentences for five of the words.

WORD BANK

producer	plankton	benthos	ocean trench	midocean ridge
consumer	photosynthesis	nekton	continental shelf	abyssal plain
reef	chemosynthesis	seamount	continental slope	

```
G Z F H V I R X J C X H Z U F Y E M J S
E O H M Y P Z R P O H F Z Z X S J I Q B
C P G P G E C F I N O Z A Z I K R D F H
O A B R P K X W R T O J P S V L C O P C
N B S O M E U M V I K H E H H T O C H U
T Y L D E M A B M N Y H M R X L N E O Z
I S I U Q N Q P C E T V L X Q A S A T U
N S N C Q J N T O N H O R Q F Q U N O R
E A E E M W K N Y T S C F Q P Z M R S P
N L O R L I Y S T A Y E L E U G E I Y T
T P H M S Q O A O L G A A D X U R D N S
A L V N N M R G R S N P M L S K G T H
L A Z R E I B E O H V T L L O Y C E H P
S I M H L K Q K M E H R N H A U G S E Q
L N C S D U T K X L P E T K D N N T S T
O I R P R W C O J F S N D X E P K T I I
P K I D C D F R N M E C W U V Q A T S Z
E K J K N B T E A B J H K T S T X Z O D
T O V U M A D E J Z E C J E E K V J X N
S Q U O E Z K F Q I M X Y P M R R L J S
```

The Living Ocean

C R O S S W O R D   P U Z Z L E

DIRECTIONS: Complete the crossword puzzle.

ACROSS

3. a colony of coral

5. process by which plants make food from sunlight

6. organisms that drift with the water currents

7. flat area that begins at the shoreline and continues until the ocean floor slopes steeply downward

8. plants and animals living on the ocean floor

9. aquatic plant-like protists that create food through photosynthesis

DOWN

1. animals that swim in the ocean, rather than drifting with the water current or staying attached to the bottom

2. begins at the edge of the continental shelf and continues down to the flattest part of the ocean floor

4. process by which sulfur or nitrogen, rather than sunlight, is used to produce food

6. organism that makes its own food

7. organism that eats other organisms

Waves and Tides

M Y S T E R Y   W O R D S

DIRECTIONS: Write each word in the correct blank below to match each word with its definition. Circle the named letter in each answer. Then, unscramble the circled letters to reveal the mystery words.

WORD BANK

moon	crest	gravity	height	wave	trough
length	breaker	spring	neap	tides	

1. _____ movement of water usually caused by wind blowing across the ocean's surface (second letter)

2. _____ object in space that pulls on water in the oceans to cause tides

3. _____ the lowest point of a wave (first letter)

4. _____ the rising and falling of the ocean surface caused by the moon's pull of gravity (third letter)

5. _____ During _____ tides, high tides are higher and low tides are lower than usual. (sixth letter)

6. _____ During _____ tides, high tides are lower and low tides are higher than usual. (first letter)

7. _____ the highest point of a wave (third letter)

8. _____ used to describe a wave that has collapsed as it approaches land (seventh letter)

9. _____ The wave _____ is the vertical distance between a crest and a trough. (third letter)

10. _____ The wave _____ is the horizontal distance between wave crests. (first letter)

11. _____ force that causes tides to occur on Earth (third letter)

MYSTERY WORDS: This is difference in the level of the ocean at a beach at high and low tides.

_____ _____ _____ _____ _____   _____ _____ _____ _____ _____

The Ocean Floor

DIAGRAM LABELING/FILL IN THE BLANKS

DIRECTIONS: Study the diagram of the ocean floor. Write each term from the word bank in the correct blank to label the diagram. Then, write each term next to its correct description below.

WORD BANK

seamount	continental shelf	midocean ridge
ocean trench	continental slope	abyssal plain

1. _____ 4. _____

2. _____ 5. _____

3. _____ 6. _____

7. _____ long, narrow crack in the ocean floor formed when one tectonic plate is forced underneath another

8. _____ area in which mountains form when tectonic plates pull apart; magma fills in the space to form new ocean crust

9. _____ begins at the edge of the continental shelf and continues down to the flattest part of the ocean floor

10. _____ the broad, flat part of the ocean floor

11. _____ flat area that begins at the shoreline and continues until the ocean floor slopes steeply downward

12. _____ volcanic mountain formed in the ocean

O C E A N S

Ocean Life Poster

I N D E P E N D E N T   R E S E A R C H

Life at each depth of the ocean is varied and unique. Many different organisms live in the top, middle, and bottom levels of water. Some types of life, called **nekton**, can swim from one level to another, while others, known as **benthos**, spend their entire lives on, in, or near the seafloor. Still others, called **plankton**, live near the surface and float from place to place as ocean currents carry them along. Some types of organisms are **producers** because they make their own food using photosynthesis. Other organisms are known as **consumers** since they must eat other organisms in order to survive.

PROCEDURE:

1. On a piece of poster board, draw a cross section of the ocean. Divide the ocean into three horizontal sections. Label the top section *plankton*, the middle section *nekton*, and the bottom section *benthos*.

2. Cut out the organisms from page 79 and glue them into the correct ocean levels on the poster.

3. Think of three organisms that are not shown on the poster. In the boxes below, draw pictures of these organisms. Or, cut pictures of these organisms from magazines and glue them into the correct ocean levels on the poster.

4. Below each picture, label the organism as either a **producer** or **consumer**.

5. Draw arrows to show how the food chain works among ocean life. Where does each organism get its food?

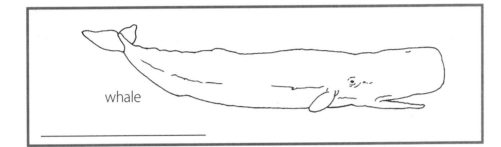

whale
_____

giant kelp
_____

shark
_____

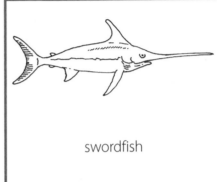

swordfish
_____

clam
_____

seal
_____

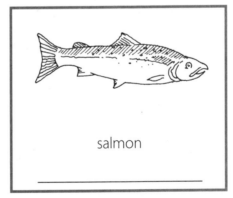

salmon
_____

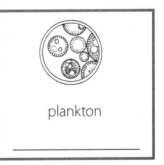

plankton
_____

jellyfish
_____

sea anemone
_____

snail
_____

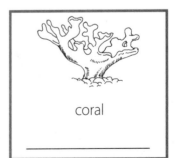

coral
_____

Ocean Pollution

Pollutants are substances that become introduced into an environment where they do not naturally occur. Examples of pollutants include trash, oil, sewage, and chemicals produced by factories. Pollutants can have a damaging effect on ocean creatures since many of these organisms are very sensitive to changes in their environment.

DIRECTIONS: Read each of the ocean pollution scenarios below. Number the events in the order that they occur.

1. _____ Algae in the ocean feed on the fertilizer, allowing them to reproduce quickly. This causes an algal bloom.

_____ The growing algae population uses most of the oxygen in the water. This causes other forms of ocean life to die from lack of oxygen.

_____ Farmers use fertilizers on their crops.

_____ Algae eventually die, and bacteria (which use up oxygen in the water) decompose the algae.

_____ Rain washes some of the fertilizer into a nearby river that eventually leads to the ocean.

2. _____ The tanker hull is punctured. Millions of gallons of oil leak into the ocean.

_____ An oil tanker runs into a coral reef in the Gulf of Mexico.

_____ Fish die because their gills become clogged with oil.

3. _____ Sea turtles, which feed on jellyfish, eat the plastic bags when they mistake them for jellyfish.

_____ Rather than using landfills for waste disposal, many countries dump trash into the ocean.

_____ The turtles die as the bags become caught in their digestive tracts.

_____ Plastic bags, full of trash, float on the surface of the ocean.

4. _____ With no trees to hold the soil in place, it gets washed by heavy rains into streams and rivers. It will eventually end up in the ocean.

_____ Huge amounts of fine soil, or silt, accumulate along the coast.

_____ When new houses are built, many trees are cut down.

_____ Young ocean animals, which live in and around the coral reefs, are covered with silt. They cannot survive and die.

_____ The silt covers coral reefs.

Name: _____ **Date:** _____

Do the Wave!

INQUIRY INVESTIGATION

Some waves are generated by wind. To see this in action, try the following activity.

MATERIALS

large plastic tub   ruler   water

three-speed fan   stopwatch

PROCEDURE:

1. Fill the plastic tub 2 cm from the top with water.

2. Place the fan 20 cm from the end of the tub. Turn it on at the lowest setting. Caution: Be sure the cord and the fan do not come in contact with any water.

3. Allow the fan to blow over the surface of the water for 2 minutes.

4. With the fan still blowing air over the water, hold the ruler vertically in the water to measure the height of the waves. Record your measurement in the table.

5. Repeat steps 3 and 4 at medium and high fan settings.

Fan Speed	Wave Height (cm)	Observations
Low		
Medium		
High		

CONCLUSIONS: Answer the following questions on a separate piece of paper.

1. In this experiment, what did the fan represent? What did the tub of water represent?

2. Is the height of a wave affected by the speed of the wind? Explain why or why not using examples from your data.

3. What are some possible sources of error in this experiment?

4. What are some other things that might affect the height of a wave? How could you test to find out if you are right?

Earth's Protective Blanket

DIRECTIONS: Find the atmosphere vocabulary words in the word search puzzle below. Words can be found across, down, and diagonally. Then, on a separate piece of paper, write sentences for five of the words.

WORD BANK

conduction	global warming	mesosphere	stratosphere
convection	greenhouse effect	ozone layer	thermosphere
exosphere	ionosphere	radiation	troposphere

```
K  P  S  X  F  W  T  M  I  O  Z  O  N  E  L  A  Y  E  R  E
T  L  B  G  V  Z  X  J  X  O  M  N  Y  R  V  X  C  B  C  S
D  L  Z  L  O  W  Z  S  V  W  N  T  H  D  U  I  Q  F  O  T
O  I  A  Z  R  L  T  T  R  O  P  O  S  P  H  E  R  E  N  R
L  G  Z  R  A  D  I  A  T  I  O  N  S  O  Q  R  R  J  V  A
F  L  C  Q  W  J  O  S  A  S  U  T  H  P  E  T  D  I  E  T
F  O  S  E  M  M  O  T  O  U  Q  H  A  R  H  T  R  A  C  O
K  B  G  R  E  E  N  H  O  U  S  E  E  F  F  E  C  T  T  S
F  A  L  I  O  R  N  G  T  C  X  H  Y  T  K  A  R  A  I  P
T  L  T  V  K  E  J  U  I  Q  P  J  M  F  R  C  Z  E  O  H
Q  W  P  Y  P  S  X  P  Z  S  J  B  G  G  K  W  M  F  N  E
V  A  B  L  L  E  C  V  O  B  B  L  G  H  L  Q  B  T  F  R
S  R  T  T  M  Q  L  X  A  J  M  E  X  I  Q  K  M  I  R  E
A  M  P  F  O  E  E  M  M  E  S  O  S  P  H  E  R  E  S  E
Y  I  T  H  E  R  M  O  S  P  H  E  R  E  N  D  R  S  J  E
F  N  U  Z  I  U  J  C  O  N  D  U  C  T  I  O  N  F  I  X
B  G  R  M  P  M  R  H  C  Y  O  Q  D  S  P  G  P  S  V  M
```

Under Pressure!

INQUIRY INVESTIGATION

Earth's atmosphere is made up of a mixture of gases that surrounds the entire planet. We cannot see it, taste it, or smell it, but we would instantly know if it suddenly was not there! Besides providing the oxygen we breathe, it maintains the **air pressure** that keeps the gases found in our blood dissolved. To understand how air pressure works, try the following investigations.

Teacher note: Before completing this activity, ask families about possible latex allergies. Also, remember that uninflated or popped balloons may present a choking hazard.

INVESTIGATION 1: Does Air Have Mass?

MATERIALS

pan or electronic balance   large balloon

PROCEDURE:

1. Place the balloon on the balance and find its mass. Record it in the table below.

2. Blow up the balloon to its maximum capacity, tie it off, and find its mass again. Record it in the table below.

Mass of Deflated Balloon (g)	Mass of Inflated Balloon (g)	Change in Mass (g)

CONCLUSIONS:

1. Describe what happened to the mass of the balloon after it was inflated.

   _____

   _____

2. Does air have mass? How do you know?

   _____

   _____

INVESTIGATION 2: The Myth of Suction

MATERIALS

glass jelly jar	water	long fireplace matches
water balloon	tealight candle	

PROCEDURE:

1. Fill a water balloon with water so that it is slightly larger than the opening of the jelly jar. Tie off the balloon.

2. Place the candle in the bottom of the jar. Have your teacher use a long fireplace match to light it.

3. Place the balloon on the opening of the jar. Observe the balloon. Draw a picture of what happens in the box below.

CONCLUSIONS:

1. Describe what happened to the balloon when it was placed on the opening of the jar.

   _____

   _____

   _____

2. Many people mistakenly believe that the balloon is "sucked" into the jar. However, this idea is incorrect. What might be another explanation for what happened? How might air pressure be involved?

   _____

   _____

WEATHER AND CLIMATE

Fronts

FILL IN THE BLANKS/DIAGRAM LABELING

DIRECTIONS: A **front** is a boundary where different air masses meet but do not mix. Write the words from the word bank in the correct blanks to match each type of front with its definition. Then, use the same words to label the front diagrams below.

WORD BANK

cold front	warm front	stationary front	occluded front

1. _____ A warm air mass slides over a cold air mass. This type of front can cause precipitation in the form of rain, sleet, or snow.

2. _____ Colder air forces warm air upward, which closes off warm air from Earth's surface.

3. _____ A cold air mass and a warm air mass move toward each other. The warm air gets lifted over the top of the cold air and forms clouds. This often results in heavy rain or snowstorms.

4. _____ Neither cold air nor warm air advances or moves. Where the two fronts meet, temperatures do not change and gentle winds occur.

5. _____   7. _____

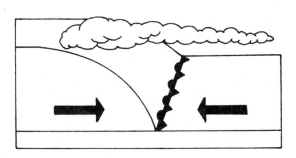

6. _____   8. _____

Station Models

Meteorologists are scientists who study and predict weather patterns. They use **station models** to show what the weather conditions are in a certain area. The symbols on a station model often appear confusing, but they are easy to understand if you have a key!

DIRECTIONS: Study the basic station model key below. This is only a sample of the many symbols that meteorologists use when reading station models. Use the key to read each of the station models on page 95. Then, write the meaning of each symbol for items 1–24.

Basic Station Model Key

Type of Precipitation	Symbol	Amount of Cloud Cover	Symbol	Wind Speed	Symbol
Snow	✳	No Cloud Cover	◯	Calm	◎
Rain	●	Scattered Clouds	◔	1–2 Knots	—
Fog	☰	Partly Cloudy	◑	3–7 Knots	⌐
Hail	▲	Mostly Cloudy	◕	8–12 Knots	∖
Thunderstorms	⚡	Overcast	●	13–17 Knots	∖

Air Temperature (°F)

Barometric Pressure (mb)

77   249

Present Precipitation

Previous Precipitation (one hour ago)

68

Dew Point (°F)

Amount of Cloud Cover

Wind Direction and Speed (knots)

HUMANS AND THE ENVIRONMENT

The Fragile Environment

WORD SEARCH

DIRECTIONS: Find the human–environmental interaction vocabulary words in the word search puzzle below. Words can be found across, down, and diagonally. Then, on a separate piece of paper, write sentences for five of the words.

WORD BANK

natural resource	renewable	acid rain	litter	nuclear energy
nonrenewable	smog	fossil fuel	compost	lumber
recycling	strip mining	petroleum	pollution	hydroelectric

```
D L O L P M S J T V J O C U I A A G H O
S N V C L E O T L O L A B Z S C C J N R
U F J C G U T E R M M C C H C I X F A H
Z T Y O P F M R V I G D U Z R D D S T W
H H K M O B B B O I P W E T B R X T U Z
L R Z P L N K G E L G M C X J A Y N R H
I A G O L Z U M G R E E I B I I O N A A
T N O S U A Z C W K L U Y N W N O R L N
T R Q T T J H R L E S N M J I U Z E R W
E T U W I W X J O E T O P S O N V N E E
R S R X O L J R W V A N M X W P G E S P
P B Q E N C D J U H I R B H D F N W O U
Q U W F C Y R A Y B X E E H B E G A U T
A F A L H Y R G S B T N S N Q C J B R P
P E E L T F C A I Y V E T N E W V L C H
V E C W W G B L Z R D W Z G J R K E E D
W T Z U O B K O I O T A V O B J G S T N
Q I I M C A K X R N D B I U J L X Y P M
O S S Q M C R C N A G L A H V B W N Y L
E F J F O S S I L F U E L T T E U T O D
```

The Fragile Environment

CROSSWORD PUZZLE

DIRECTIONS: Complete the crossword puzzle.

ACROSS

1. nonrenewable energy resource that forms from buried remains of organisms
5. _____ involves removing rock and soil from Earth's surface to expose materials to be mined.
7. A _____ natural resource can never be replaced or can only be replaced over thousands of year.
8. liquid fossil fuel or oil

DOWN

2. thick, brown photochemical fog that is formed when sunlight reacts with gases from air pollution
3. _____ is caused by air pollution containing sulfur dioxide.
4. A _____ natural resource can be used and then replaced over a short period of time.
6. the process by which used items are treated and reused
7. A _____ resource is any substance, organism, or energy used by living things that occurs in nature.

Is Your Rain Acidic?

Air pollution causes many environmental problems, including smog and depletion of the ozone layer. In addition, air pollution can cause a problem known as acid rain. **Acid rain** is moisture with a pH below 5.6 that falls to Earth's surface. **pH** is a measure of how acidic or basic a substance is. The pH scale ranges from 0–14, as shown in the figure below.

0	1	2	3	4	5	6	7	8	9	10	11	12	13	14

battery acid   vinegar   tomatoes   baking soda   ammonia   bleach

Any substance below 7.0 on the pH scale is an **acid**, while any substance above 7.0 is a **base**. A substance closer to either end of the scale is a stronger acid or base than substances that are closer to the middle of the scale. Substances in the middle of the scale are **neutral**. In order to learn about the pH of common household substances, try the following investigation.

MATERIALS

pH paper or pH meter	liquid laundry detergent	precipitation (snow or rain) from your area
distilled water	carbonated soft drink	
lemon juice	milk	9 small plastic cups
antacid tablet	seawater or highly concentrated salt water	permanent marker
window cleaner		graduated cylinder

PROCEDURE:

1. Label each cup with the name of the substance it will contain. Pour 10 mL of each substance in a cup. To prepare the antacid tablet, dissolve it in 10 mL of distilled water.

2. Predict the pH of each substance. Record your predictions in the data table on page 106.

3. Test the pH of each substance by dipping the pH paper or meter into each substance. Record the actual pH of each substance in the data table.

DATA TABLE:

Substance	Prediction of pH	Actual pH
distilled water		
lemon juice		
dissolved antacid tablet		
window cleaner		
liquid laundry detergent		
carbonated soft drink		
milk		
seawater or highly concentrated salt water		
precipitation from your area		

RESULTS:

1. Which items are acidic? Basic? Neutral?

Acidic: _____

_____

Basic: _____

_____

Neutral: _____

_____

CONCLUSION:

2. Was the precipitation you collected acidic? How do you know?

_____

_____

_____

Name: _____   Date: _____

Our Home Planet Earth

DIRECTIONS: Complete the crossword puzzle.

ACROSS

4. length of time for Earth to orbit the sun once

7. an orbit around the sun

8. property of Earth that causes seasons

9. shape of Earth's orbit

10. imaginary line around which Earth spins

12. When the sun is directly over this imaginary line, daytime hours equal nighttime hours.

DOWN

1. round, three-dimensional object; shape of the Earth

2. length of time for Earth to spin on its axis once

3. occurs when the sun reaches its greatest distance north or south of the equator

5. occurs when the sun is directly over the equator

6. When the northern hemisphere is tilted away from the sun, it is this season in North America.

7. Earth's spinning that causes day and night

11. When the northern hemisphere is tilted toward the sun, it is this season in North America.

SUN-EARTH-MOON RELATIONSHIPS

Earth's Satellite

WORD SEARCH

DIRECTIONS: Find the sun-Earth-moon system vocabulary words in the word search puzzle below. Words can be found across, down, and diagonally. Then, on a separate piece of paper, write sentences for five of the words.

WORD BANK

first quarter	moon phases	crescent	third quarter	maria	revolution	solstice
waxing	new moon	full moon	gibbous	axis	rotation	ellipse
month	lunar eclipse	solar eclipse	waning	equinox	tilt	equator

```
L  A  M  O  N  T  H  V  R  T  D  Y  H  F  E  C  V  J  L  P
U  C  W  E  I  Z  A  H  N  G  Q  Y  P  U  C  O  F  A  R  W
N  A  Z  Y  B  Y  Y  E  A  K  M  G  H  L  X  T  T  S  O  G
A  E  X  G  C  T  C  I  T  A  D  I  F  L  R  H  X  N  T  Z
R  F  R  N  T  S  W  B  S  Z  D  B  Q  M  W  I  S  D  A  U
E  A  A  M  E  T  I  L  T  Y  M  B  Z  O  X  R  O  R  T  K
C  B  T  R  I  T  W  R  K  J  C  O  P  O  W  D  L  E  I  U
L  L  C  A  M  C  Z  R  V  U  E  U  D  N  E  Q  A  V  O  F
I  S  A  Z  E  D  A  A  Q  S  P  S  O  C  Q  U  R  O  N  I
P  Y  X  I  Y  Q  M  Q  P  F  V  C  T  G  U  A  E  L  M  R
S  Y  I  A  O  N  U  I  V  Z  F  B  Z  S  I  R  C  U  A  S
E  R  S  Q  H  Q  L  A  Q  O  E  D  W  S  N  T  L  T  R  T
Z  C  G  V  Q  L  J  X  T  W  C  L  N  O  O  E  I  I  I  Q
A  X  Q  K  E  G  D  O  K  O  A  T  B  E  X  R  P  O  A  U
V  Q  K  E  Q  X  O  W  Z  X  R  N  U  Z  W  F  S  N  R  A
A  E  J  T  M  N  J  C  A  I  R  E  I  B  K  M  E  K  I  R
M  S  O  L  S  T  I  C  E  X  S  Q  F  N  L  R  O  C  A  T
L  E  L  C  O  B  E  W  T  G  I  R  U  B  G  M  B  O  T  E
X  W  R  C  I  H  U  Q  Q  X  R  N  I  G  E  H  Z  L  N  R
M  O  O  N  P  H  A  S  E  S  A  G  G  J  E  Y  Q  K  N  E
```

Name: _____   Date: _____

Earth's Satellite

DIRECTIONS: Complete the crossword puzzle.

ACROSS

1. moon phase when none of the lighted side can be seen

4. occurs when Earth is directly between the sun and moon, blocking sunlight to the moon

8. moon phase when all of the lighted side can be seen

9. the amount of the lighted side of the moon appears to be increasing

12. approximate period of time it takes for the moon to orbit Earth once

13. moon phase when only half of the lighted side can be seen; occurs after a full moon

DOWN

2. period after a full moon when the amount of the lighted side of the moon appears to be decreasing

3. dark, flat regions of dry lava on the surface of the moon

5. moon phase when only a sliver of light can be seen

6. occurs when the moon moves directly between Earth and the sun, which causes a shadow over part of the Earth

7. moon phase when half of the lighted side can be seen; occurs after a new moon

10. changing appearance of the moon as seen from Earth

11. moon phase when three-quarters of the lighted side can be seen

Sun-Earth-Moon System

DIRECTIONS: Study the diagram of the sun-Earth-moon system. Then, answer the questions below. The small lettered circles represent the moon in four different positions as it revolves around the Earth during the course of one month. Keep in mind that this diagram is not to scale.

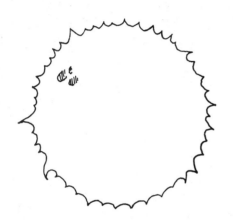
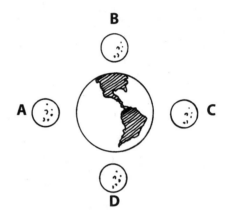

1. In which position would the moon need to be in order for a person on Earth to observe a full moon?

   Position _____

2. In which position would the moon need to be in order for a person on Earth to observe a solar eclipse?

   Position _____

3. The moon would need to be in between which two positions in order for a person on Earth to observe a crescent moon?

   Position _____ and _____

4. In which position would the moon need to be in order for a person on Earth to observe a lunar eclipse?

   Position _____

5. With the moon in position A, it is called a new moon. As the moon moves to position B, more of the moon's lighted surface becomes visible. This period of the moon cycle is called:

   a. gibbous   b. solstice   c. waxing   d. waning

Name: _____   Date: _____

To the Moon!

In 1961, President John F. Kennedy announced that the United States would attempt to land a man on the moon and return him safely to Earth. In order to accomplish this, NASA created three space programs: Mercury, Gemini, and Apollo. Each program was a small stepping stone toward accomplishing the final goal of landing on the moon.

DIRECTIONS: Use science books, encyclopedias, or the Internet to research each of these programs. Then, in the space below, write a summary of each program, including its goals and accomplishments.

1. Mercury: _____

_____

_____

_____

_____

2. Gemini: _____

_____

_____

_____

_____

_____

3. Apollo: _____

_____

_____

_____

_____

_____

S U N - E A R T H - M O O N   R E L A T I O N S H I P S

Solar and Lunar Eclipses

D I A G R A M   L A B E L I N G

An eclipse can occur when the light of the sun becomes blocked by the moon or Earth. Two types of shadows can be observed during an eclipse: an umbra and a penumbra. The **umbra** is the darkest part of a shadow. If you are standing in the umbra, the source of light is completely blocked by the object causing the shadow. This is different from the **penumbra**, in which the light source is only partially blocked and there is only a partial shadow.

DIRECTIONS: Follow the directions below to create a diagram of an eclipse. Then, answer the questions that follow. Keep in mind that this diagram is not to scale.

1. Use a ruler to draw two straight lines from point **A** on the sun through points **C** and **D** on the moon. Stop the lines when they strike the edge of Earth.

2. Draw two additional straight lines from point **B** on the sun through points **C** and **D** on the moon. Stop the lines when they strike the edge of Earth.

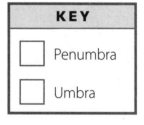

3. Name the type of eclipse pictured in the diagram. _____

4. During which phase of the moon would this type of eclipse occur?

   _____

5. Use a colorful pencil to shade in the **umbra**. Using a different color, shade in the **penumbra**. Show what colors you used in the key.

6. If you were observing this eclipse from Earth, in which part of the shadow would you need to be to observe a total eclipse?

   _____

7. Use the Internet to find out when you may be able to view this type of eclipse.

8. Use a ruler to draw a straight line from point **A** on the sun through point **C** on Earth. Stop the line when it passes the edge of the moon.

9. Draw a second line from point **B** on the sun through point **D** on Earth. Stop the line when it passes the edge of the moon.

10. Name the type of eclipse pictured in the diagram. _____

11. During which phase of the moon would this type of eclipse occur?

_____

12. If you were able to see this eclipse from Earth, what time of day would it be?

_____

13. Explain why you think Earth does not experience a lunar eclipse every month.

_____

_____

_____

14. Two planets in our solar system do not experience lunar or solar eclipses. Name the planets and explain why they do not experience any eclipses.

_____

_____

_____

15. Use the Internet to find out when you may be able to view this type of eclipse.

SUN-EARTH-MOON RELATIONSHIPS

Modeling Moon Phases

INQUIRY INVESTIGATION

A **model** is one way scientists explain the way in which something works. In this activity, you will view all of the moon phases within a few minutes, rather than completing actual moon observations over the course of one month.

MATERIALS

| plastic foam ball | flashlight or overhead projector | pencil |

PROCEDURE:

1. Poke the pencil into the plastic foam ball so that it makes a handle.

2. Turn on the flashlight or overhead projector and turn off any lights in the room. Then, stand facing the flashlight or projector. The light represents the sun, the ball represents the moon, and your head represents Earth.

3. Hold the moon ball in your left hand slightly above your head. Although the light should be shining in your eyes, you should not be able to see any light reflected off the moon. This is called a **new moon**, and it occurs when the moon is between Earth and the sun. It is shown in the chart below.

4. Slowly turn your body to the left in a counterclockwise direction. Keep your eyes on the moon ball. You will see a tiny sliver of light reflected on the moon's surface. This is called a **waxing crescent moon**. It is shown in the chart below.

5. As you continue moving your body in a counterclockwise direction, you will view each moon phase. Draw how the moon appears at each phase in the chart below.

New Moon	Waxing Crescent	First Quarter	Waxing Gibbous	Full Moon	Waning Gibbous	Third Quarter	Waning Crescent
◯	◐	◯	◯	◯	◯	◯	◯

6. Return to the new moon position. This time, position the moon directly between your head and the sun so that it blocks light from reaching your face. Which type of eclipse is this?

_____

7. Next, turn your body to the full moon position, but this time, place the moon directly in line with your head. Which type of eclipse is this?

_____

Name: _____   Date: _____

Our Solar System

WORD SEARCH

DIRECTIONS: Find the solar system vocabulary words in the word search puzzle below. Words can be found across, down, and diagonally. Then, on a separate piece of paper, write sentences for five of the words.

WORD BANK

Oort cloud	Uranus	sun	Mercury	comet
Jupiter	Great Red Spot	*Viking*	Venus	methane
Neptune	Pluto	Earth	Mars	
Saturn	meteorite	asteroid belt	astronomical unit	
Voyager	Olympus Mons	Luna		

```
O  I  L  R  G  A  G  B  U  V  P  N  X  S  A  L  M  X  I  J
M  H  A  S  A  T  U  R  N  G  L  M  A  W  O  B  B  X  M  G
V  L  S  V  D  Y  H  X  E  E  U  W  A  I  U  R  A  N  U  S
C  B  T  W  E  N  W  I  P  H  T  O  G  Y  Z  H  C  N  A  V
O  C  E  C  B  N  C  W  T  U  O  I  R  G  L  T  O  Z  W  Y
O  Q  R  Q  P  J  U  R  U  Z  M  V  A  G  D  B  M  W  X  T
R  T  O  O  D  E  A  S  N  X  L  L  O  S  B  W  E  S  Y  A
T  F  I  M  O  E  Z  A  E  O  P  M  N  Y  G  V  T  S  U  J
C  W  D  E  E  B  T  C  T  F  G  O  E  N  A  P  S  R  G  N
L  O  B  R  H  T  U  N  R  V  M  U  H  T  C  G  E  V  R  K
O  N  E  C  G  D  E  D  J  S  S  U  C  D  H  T  E  C  E  L
U  Q  L  U  W  J  E  O  U  E  B  C  Y  Y  I  A  Q  R  A  K
D  U  T  R  X  V  G  P  R  J  C  B  X  P  L  A  N  N  T  M
L  K  D  Y  R  U  M  G  P  I  Q  G  U  K  Z  D  U  E  R  P
V  B  Y  S  E  Y  Y  L  R  U  T  J  L  N  Y  L  Y  J  E  E
I  P  K  P  L  H  P  L  J  T  D  E  M  A  R  S  E  J  D  T
K  X  P  O  M  B  S  U  G  P  I  F  Y  J  V  S  G  N  S  M
I  A  S  T  R  O  N  O  M  I  C  A  L  U  N  I  T  H  P  Y
N  Z  V  C  N  X  Q  E  Z  P  C  V  E  L  D  L  J  M  O  R
G  U  K  O  M  Z  C  F  F  G  L  D  A  V  R  U  Q  O  T  D
```

Inner Solar System

DIRECTIONS: Complete the crossword puzzle.

ACROSS

3. often called the "red planet"

5. separates the inner planets from the outer planets

7. spacecraft that landed on Mars in the 1970s

8. largest volcano in the solar system

DOWN

1. name of Earth's moon

2. planet with an atmosphere that consists mainly of nitrogen and oxygen

3. planet closet to the sun

4. number of moons orbiting Mercury and Venus

6. this object in space contains over 99% of the mass of the solar system

7. sometimes called "Earth's twin"

Name: _____   Date: _____

Outer Solar System

DIRECTIONS: Complete the crossword puzzle.

ACROSS

3. planet with an orbit that intersects the orbit of the dwarf planet Pluto

5. area of the solar system in which comets are located

6. planet with the largest ring system

8. huge storm on Jupiter

DOWN

1. largest planet in the solar system

2. planet that rotates on its side

4. spacecraft that flew by and photographed the four gas giants in the 1970s

7. gas that gives Neptune and Uranus their blue-green color

8. all outer planets are composed mainly of this type of matter

9. moon of Jupiter; possibly contains a liquid ocean under its surface

10. space object that was reclassified as a dwarf planet in 2006

SOLAR SYSTEM

Solar System Distances

MATH SKILLS

An **astronomical unit (AU)** is the average distance between Earth and the sun. One astronomical unit equals approximately 93 million miles. Astronomical units are used to measure distances in our solar system because of the great distances between the planets.

DIRECTIONS: Complete the table below to show the distance between the sun and each planet in miles and astronomical units. Mercury has been completed for you.

Planet	Distance from the Sun (miles)	Distance from the Sun (AUs)
Mercury	37.2 million miles	0.4 AU
Venus		0.7 AU
Earth	93 million miles	
Mars		1.5 AU
Jupiter		5.2 AU
Saturn	883.5 million miles	
Uranus		19.2 AU
Neptune	2,790 million miles	

SOLAR SYSTEM

Which Planet Am I?

FILL IN THE BLANKS

DIRECTIONS: Write each name of a planet from the word bank in the correct blank below to match the planet with a description. Each planet will be used twice.

WORD BANK

Jupiter	Earth	Neptune	Mercury
Venus	Uranus	Mars	Saturn

1. _____ planet with the largest volcano in the solar system

2. _____ planet with an atmosphere that rains sulfuric acid

3. _____ planet that rotates on its side

4. _____ planet with the most extreme temperature range (700°F to -300°F)

5. _____ planet that is one astronomical unit (AU) from the sun

6. _____ largest planet in the solar system

7. _____ only planet known to support life

8. _____ planet with an atmosphere that has an extreme greenhouse effect

9. _____ planet with iron oxide in its soil, giving it a red appearance

10. _____ planet that has an orbit that intersects the orbit of the dwarf planet Pluto

11. _____ planet with the Great Red Spot

12. _____ planet with the largest rings

13. _____ planet with a density so low that it could float on water

14. _____ only inner planet with no atmosphere

15. _____ the two planets with methane in their atmospheres, giving them a blue-green color

_____

Planetary Missions

Scientists and engineers who design space missions must take many things into account. The type of research that will be conducted during the mission will determine which type of mission is used.

A **flyby mission** involves sending a spacecraft past the planet, usually to take pictures on its way to another planet. The *Voyager* missions of the 1970s were flyby missions, and they returned some of the first close-up images of the outer planets.

An **orbiter mission** requires more complex instrumentation and engineering than a flyby. Its purpose is to orbit the planet or moon for an extended period of time in order to map the surface, conduct atmospheric analysis, and scout locations for future lander missions.

A **robotic lander mission** actually lands a spacecraft in a predetermined location in order to conduct an in-depth study of a certain area. These missions often have specific scientific objectives that can be achieved by up-close observation. These spacecraft are highly complex with specialized instruments and computers.

The only **human mission** to an object in space occurred in the late 1960s and early 1970s when humans landed on the moon. Human missions are very dangerous, but they allow highly in-depth studies of the planet or moon.

PROCEDURE:

1. Before class, obtain a ball (a basketball, soccer ball, or kick ball). Decorate it with stickers, buttons, charms, and other interesting items. This will be a new "planet" that several types of missions will explore. Before class, cover the ball with a towel and place it in the center of the room.

2. Give each student a copy of the activity on pages 121 and 122. Introduce the four main types of missions to students. Ask them to guess the purpose of each mission based on its name, followed by discussion.

3. **Flyby mission:** Uncover the planet and tell students to walk past it in single file. After they walk by, they should record on the data sheet (page 121) their observations about what they saw on the planet. Encourage students to draw a picture of the planet as well.

4. **Orbiter mission:** Students will walk in a circle around the planet for one minute. After they orbit the planet, they should record their observations and drawings on the data sheet.

5. **Robotic lander mission:** Students should choose an area of the planet they would like to study more closely. Allow students to take turns looking at the area they chose through a paper-towel tube for one minute. Remind them that once scientists land the robotic lander on the planet, it is not easy to move it to another location. So, once they have chosen their areas, they may not choose others!

6. Based on their experiences in this simulation, students should answer questions 7–14 (page 122). These can be assigned as homework or discussed as a group in class.

Planetary Missions

1. Describe each type of mission below.

Flyby: _____

_____

Orbiter: _____

_____

Robotic lander: _____

_____

Human: _____

_____

2. Conduct a flyby of the "planet" shown to you by your teacher. Record observations and draw a picture of the planet.

_____

_____

_____

3. Orbit the "planet" for one minute. Record observations and draw a picture of the planet.

_____

_____

_____

4. Choose a place on the "planet" to land a robotic spacecraft. Examine this area through a paper-towel tube. Record observations and draw a picture of this area of the planet.

_____

_____

_____

5. If there were humans aboard a spacecraft that landed in the area you chose, how might their observations be different from the robotic lander's observations?

_____

_____

_____

6. What are the advantages and disadvantages of each type of mission?

Mission	Advantages	Disadvantages
flyby		
orbiter		
robotic lander		
human		

Listed below are scientific questions about the planets and moons in our solar system. Name the type of mission that could be used to answer each space exploration question.

7. What types of volcanoes exist on the entire surface of Mars? _____

8. Can the mineral hematite be found on the surface of Mars? _____

9. Are there fossilized life forms on Mars? _____

10. What does the surface of Pluto look like? _____

11. What types of gases compose Jupiter, Saturn, Uranus, and Neptune? _____

12. Can plants grown on the surface of Mars be used as a food source? _____

13. Are rocks on Mercury similar to rocks found on Earth? _____

14. How do the landforms in the northern and southern hemispheres of Venus compare?

_____

Scientists Who Study the Earth (page 9)

1. seismologist
2. meteorologist
3. oceanographer
4. paleontologist
5. cartographer
6. gemologist
7. hydrogeologist
8. volcanologist
9. geochemist
10. planetary geologist
11. climatologist
12. petroleum geologist

Elements in Earth's Crust (page 10)

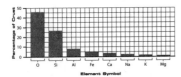

1. 98.5%
2. 1.5%
3. 74.3%

Meet the Minerals (page 11)

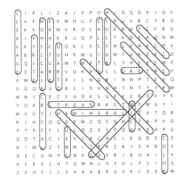

Meet the Minerals (page 12)

ACROSS
3. color
4. quartz
8. halite
9. calcite

12. cleavage
13. pyrite
14. luster

DOWN
1. graphite
2. magnetite
5. talc
6. mica

7. sulfur
10. hardness
11. streak

Which Mineral Am I? (page 13)

1. sulfur
2. graphite
3. galena

4. quartz
5. magnetite
6. talc

Mineral Matching (page 14)

1. g
2. f
3. b
4. h

5. a
6. c
7. i
8. d

9. l
10. e
11. m
12. j

13. n
14. k

Mystery Word: acid

Minerals All around Us (page 15)

Answers will vary.

Minerals Rock! (page 16)

1. cleavage
2. streak
3. color
4. hardness
5. fracture
6. graphite

7. halite
8. talc
9. magnetite
10. luster
11. gems

Mystery Word: hematite

Magic Crystals (page 17)

1. Answers will vary.
2. Answers will vary.
3. When the water evaporated, the crystals were left behind in the bowls.
4. Crystals form when water containing minerals evaporates, leaving the minerals behind.

Igneous, Sedimentary, or Metamorphic? (page 19)

1. M
2. S
3. S
4. I
5. S

6. I
7. I
8. M
9. S
10. M

11. S
12. I
13. I
14. M
15. I

16. S
17. I
18. M
19. S
20. I

Simply Sedimentary (page 20)

ACROSS
1. clastic
3. chemical
4. weathering
6. organic

8. conglomerate
9. sedimentary
10. shale

DOWN
1. cementation
2. stratification
3. compaction

5. fossils
7. limestone

The Pressure on Metamorphic Rocks (page 21)

1. metamorphic
2. foliated
3. nonfoliated
4. sedimentary
5. pressure

6. sculptures
7. magma
8. grains
9. slate

Mystery Word: Lincoln

Which Rock Am I? (page 22)

1. conglomerate
2. granite
3. slate

4. obsidian
5. limestone
6. marble

The Rock Cycle (page 23)

1. melting and crystallization
2. heating and pressure
3. heating and pressure
4. sedimentation and compaction
5. melting and crystallization
6. sedimentation and compaction

A "Rock"-ing Autobiography (page 24)

Stories will vary.

Modeling Rocks (page 25)

3. sedimentary
5. igneous
7. metamorphic
8. Answers will vary but may include that it is similar because it models how different types of rocks form and change. It is different because the actual rock cycle takes millions of years to complete.

The Weathering of Earth (page 27)

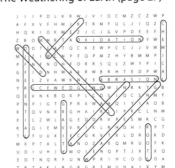

The Weathering of Earth (page 28)

ACROSS
2. weathering
4. oxidation
7. gravity
8. chemical

9. ice wedging
11. wind
12. roots

DOWN
1. differential
3. acid
5. abrasion

6. mechanical
10. water

Mechanical or Chemical? (page 29)

1. C
2. M
3. M

4. C
5. M
6. C

7. M
8. C
9. M

10. M

Mechanical Weathering (page 30)

1. The rock's mass should get smaller as the experiment progresses.
2. Answers will vary.
3. Tiny pieces of rock fragments were broken off by the action of water and the bottle.
4. In nature, rocks can be mechanically weathered by tumbling along river bottoms and streambeds.
5. Graphs will vary.

What's in Our Soil? (page 32)

1. h   4. c   7. d
2. a   5. e   8. i
3. f   6. g   9. b

Magic Number = 15

Over the Horizon (page 33)

1. horizon O   7. horizon R
2. horizon A   8. horizon C
3. horizon B   9. horizon A
4. horizon C   10. horizon B
5. horizon R   11. horizon A
6. horizon B   12. horizon O

Fascinating Fossils (page 34)

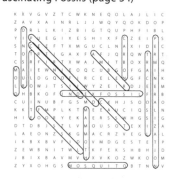

Fascinating Fossils (page 35)

ACROSS
2. mold   8. permineralization
4. index   9. amber
DOWN
1. fossil   6. cast
3. petrified   7. carbon
5. trace

Unconformities (page 36)

1. b   2. a   3. c
4. angular unconformity
5. disconformity
6. nonconformity

Layers of Rock (page 37)

Cross section 1: H E D C G F B A
Cross section 2: A F B G E C D

Millions of Years Ago . . . (page 38)

Answers are approximate.
1. 303 pages   3. 11,817 pages
2. 19,695 pages   4. 60,600 pages

A Paleontology Puzzle (page 40)

1. *Tyrannosaurus rex*
2. Answers will vary but may include that it is similar because scientists often find skeletal remains that they must piece together based on prior knowledge. It is different because scientists would have to be careful as they dig out actual skeletons.
3. anatomy—so that they can know how the structure fits together
   geology—so that they can know each type of rock and the ages of fossils found in those rocks
4. They would have to be able to separate and identify each type of animal skeleton.

Earth's Shifting Surface (page 42)

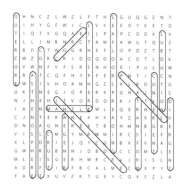

Earth's Shifting Surface (page 43)

ACROSS
3. mantle   8. lithosphere
4. Wegener   9. inner core
6. plates   10. continental drift
7. outer core
DOWN
1. asthenosphere 5. crust
2. spreading

The Puzzle of Pangaea (page 44)

A Controversial Idea (page 45)

Speeches will vary.

Know Your Boundaries (page 46)

1. c   4. a   7. e
2. d   5. f
3. g   6. b

8. convergent or continental collision
9. transform
10. divergent/rift valley
11. subduction

Inside the Earth (page 47)

1. crust   7. outer core
2. lithosphere   8. crust
3. asthenosphere 9. mantle
4. mantle   10. lithosphere
5. outer core   11. inner core
6. inner core   12. asthenosphere

A Current Event (page 48)

1. Answers will vary but may include: When the water reached the sides of the dish, it heated up and rose to the surface. Once at the surface, the water would move to the center and sink.
2. Answer will vary but may include: When the hot plate heated the water, it caused it to rise. When the water cooled at the surface, it sank back down to the bottom of the dish.

Quaking, Shaking Earth (page 49)

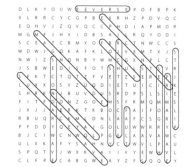

Quaking, Shaking Earth (page 50)

ACROSS
3. seismology   7. magnitude
5. secondary   8. epicenter
6. seismograph
DOWN
1. fault   4. focus
2. primary   5. seismic
3. surface

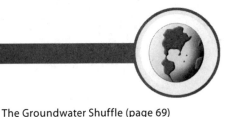

Earthquake Travel Times (page 51)

1. 5 min.
2. about 4 min.
3. about 1,500 km
4. about 700 km
5. P wave
6. time difference increases
7. about 1,500 km

Earthquake Locations (page 52)

1. Most epicenters are found on or near plate boundaries. These are areas of high seismic activity.
2. Earthquakes would likely occur along plate boundaries; plate movements can cause earthquakes.
3. People may be safer on the interior of plates; only occasionally does seismic activity occur there.
4. It can help predict future occurrences of earthquakes.

Whose "Fault" Is It? (page 54)

1. normal
2. strike-slip
3. reverse
4. strike-slip
5. normal
6. reverse

Quaking Elsewhere! (page 55)

Answers will vary.

Shakedown! (page 56)

1. The skyscraper was not built to resist the vibrations of the falling dictionary.
2. Answers will vary.
3. Answers will vary.

Earth's Cooling Vents (page 58)

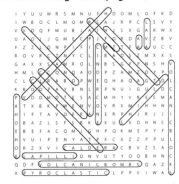

Earth's Cooling Vents (page 59)

ACROSS
5. composite
8. lava
9. hot spot
10. crater
DOWN
1. shield
2. pyroclastic
3. volcano
4. rift
5. cinder cone
6. magma
7. caldera

Flowing Eruptions (page 60)

1. pahoehoe
2. aa
3. pillow
4. volcanic bombs
5. volcanic blocks
6. lapilli
7. volcanic ash
Mystery Word: Hawaii

Movement Inside the Earth (page 61)

1. sill
2. dike
3. volcanic neck
4. batholith
5. volcanic neck
6. sill
7. dike
8. batholith

Otherworldly Volcanoes (page 62)

Letters will vary.

Lava in the Lab—Part 1 (page 63)

1. Answers will vary.
2. Answers will vary.
3. Actual lava will flow at different rates depending on many different variables, including the height and slope of the volcano and the temperature of the lava.

Lava in the Lab—Part 2 (page 65)

Investigations will vary.

A Cycle of Water (page 66)

1. evaporation
2. condensation
3. precipitation
4. runoff
5. infiltration
6. transpiration
7. precipitation
8. condensation
9. infiltration
10. runoff
11. evaporation
10. transpiration

Rivers and Streams (page 67)

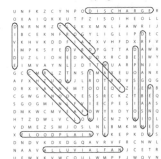

Rivers and Streams (page 68)

ACROSS
1. drainage basin
2. divide
3. water cycle
6. floodplain
7. tributary
9. channel
11. meander
12. load
DOWN
1. discharge
2. deposition
4. alluvial fan
5. erosion
8. runoff
10. delta

The Groundwater Shuffle (page 69)

2. h
4. a
6. f
8. c
10. e
12. g
14. d
16. i
18. b
Magic number = 30

Stream Stages (page 70)

1. old stream; It is wide and flat with strong meanders and deposits sediment into a delta.
2. mature stream; It has curved meanders.
3. young stream; It has waterfalls that flow into rapids.

Speeding Streams and Rivers—Part 1 (page 71)

1. 4 m/sec.
2. 0.5 m/sec.
3. 10 m/sec.
4. 10 seconds

5. river 3 because its speed is fastest, and young rivers usually move swiftly
6. river 2 because its speed is slowest, and old rivers move very slowly

Speeding Streams and Rivers—Part 2 (page 72)

1. It would be difficult to toss the orange into the stream at exactly the 10-meter mark, so it is easier to let it float to that mark.
2. in case errors are made
3. Answers will vary.
4. Answers will vary but may include mistakes in measuring the distance and timing. The oranges may also get caught on and slowed down by other objects in the stream.

The Life and Times of a Water Droplet (page 73)

Stories will vary.

The Living Ocean (page 74)

The Living Ocean (page 75)

ACROSS

3. reef
5. photosynthesis
6. plankton

7. continental shelf
8. benthos
9. algae

DOWN

1. nekton
2. continental slope
4. chemosynthesis

6. producer
7. consumer

Waves and Tides (page 76)

1. wave
2. moon
3. trough
4. tides
5. spring
6. neap

7. crest
8. breaker
9. height
10. length
11. gravity

Mystery Word: tidal range

The Ocean Floor (page 77)

1. continental shelf
2. continental slope
3. midocean ridge
4. abyssal plain
5. ocean trench
6. seamount
7. ocean trench
8. midocean ridge
9. continental slope
10. abyssal plain
11. continental shelf
12. seamount

Ocean Life Poster (page 78)

whale, nekton, consumer
seal, nekton, consumer
shark, nekton, consumer
jellyfish, plankton, consumer
single-cell algae, plankton, producer
clam, benthos, consumer
coral, benthos, consumer
snail, benthos, consumer
sea anemone, benthos, consumer
giant kelp, benthos, producer
swordfish, nekton, consumer
salmon, nekton, consumer

Ocean Pollution (page 80)

1. 3, 4, 1, 5, 2
2. 2, 1, 3

3. 3, 1, 4, 2
4. 2, 3, 1, 5, 4

Do the Wave! (page 81)

1. fan—wind
   tub of water—body of water
2. Student data should show the higher the wind speed, the greater the height of the waves.

3. Errors could be made in measuring the wave heights or by having a malfunctioning fan.
4. Answers will vary.

Earth's Protective Blanket (page 82)

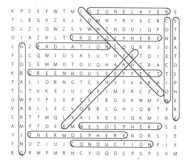

Earth's Protective Blanket (page 83)

ACROSS

1. stratosphere
7. thermosphere
9. mesosphere

10. ozone
11. conduction

DOWN

2. exosphere
3. convection
4. greenhouse
5. global warming

6. ionosphere
7. troposphere
8. radiation

Way Up in the Sky (page 84)

1. exosphere
2. thermosphere
3. mesosphere
4. stratosphere
5. troposphere

6. thermosphere
7. troposphere
8. mesosphere
9. stratosphere
10. exosphere

Graphing the Atmosphere (page 85)

1. The temperature decreases.

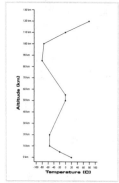

2. The temperature increases.
3. Greenhouse gases are found in the thermosphere, and these gases absorb radiation from the sun. Therefore, this layer is warmer.

Is the Earth Heating Up? (page 86)

Projects will vary but should provide detailed information for the three criteria.

Under Pressure! (page 87)

Does Air Have Mass?

1. The balance should tip toward the inflated balloon because its mass increased.
2. Air does have mass, although not much. This should be apparent in the experiment, provided the balance is sensitive enough. The mass of air is what causes air pressure to exist—the more air we have pushing on us, the greater the air pressure.

The Myth of Suction

1. The balloon should fall into the jar even though it is seemingly too large to do so.
2. The candle uses up the oxygen inside the jar (the flame will eventually go out once the balloon covers the opening), making the air pressure outside the jar greater than the pressure inside. The pressure pushing the balloon down is greater than that pushing up. So, the balloon is actually pushed, not sucked, into the jar.

Screening the Sun (page 89)

1. the bead covered with the highest SPF sunscreen
2. Answers will vary but may include that the bead covered with the highest SPF sunscreen remained the lightest in color.
3. Answers will vary but may include that the higher the SPF rating, the more effective the sunscreen is in blocking UV radiation.
4. people who are outdoors for long periods of time

Patterns of Weather (page 91)

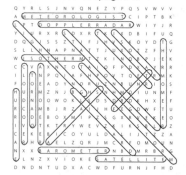

Patterns of Weather (page 92)

ACROSS

1. thunderstorm
3. hurricane
4. blizzard
7. front

9. tornado
10. air mass
11. thermometer
12. meteorologist

DOWN

2. thunder
5. lightning

6. barometer
8. anemometer

Fronts (page 93)

1. warm front
2. occluded front
3. cold front
4. stationary front

5. warm front
6. stationary front
7. cold front
8. occluded front

Station Models (page 94)

1. snow
2. 31°F
3. scattered clouds
4. 247 mb
5. southeast
6. 29°F
7. rain
8. 42°F
9. overcast
10. east
11. 13–17 knots
12. 37°F

13. rain
14. 80°F
15. partly cloudy
16. 223 mb
17. northwest
18. rain
19. thunderstorms
20. 48°F
21. mostly cloudy
22. hail
23. southwest
24. 41°F

Climactic Clues (page 96)

ACROSS

1. temperate
5. desert
7. weather
8. El Niño

10. prevailing
11. climate
12. rain forest

DOWN

2. polar
3. tundra
4. latitude

6. savanna
8. elevation
9. tropics

In the Zone (page 97)

1. tropics
2. temperate
3. polar
4. rain forest

5. desert
6. savanna
7. tundra
8. global warming

Mystery Word: evergreen

Global Climates (page 98)

1. yes because it took a few minutes for the globe to heat up
2. Temperature readings and differences will vary, but the reading at the pole should be a higher temperature. Light strikes the poles at an angle compared to the equator, which is hit directly.

3. The temperature would be higher but still not as high as the equator.
4. Different areas of Earth receive varying amounts of solar radiation, creating different climate zones.

The Fragile Environment (page 99)

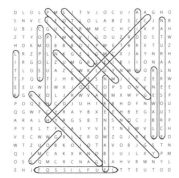

The Fragile Environment (page 100)

ACROSS

1. fossil fuel
5. strip mining

7. nonrenewable
8. petroleum

DOWN

2. smog
3. acid rain
4. renewable

6. recycling
7. natural

A Fair Share of Resources? (page 101)

1. steel
2. Answers will vary.
3. Answers will vary.

Alternative Resources (page 102)

1. nuclear
2. solar
3. hydroelectric
4. wind

5. geothermal
6. biomass
7. gasohol
8. garbage

Mystery Word: solar cell

An Energy Alternative (page 103)

Answers will vary based on student research.

Sources of Air Pollution (page 104)

1. 100%
2. industry and power plants
3. Answers will vary.

Is Your Rain Acidic? (page 105)

1. basic: detergent, antacid, window cleaner, and salt water
   acidic: lemon juice, soft drink, and milk
   neutral: distilled water
2. Answers will vary; rain is considered acidic if its pH is below 5.6.

Our Home Planet Earth (page 107)

ACROSS

4. year
7. revolution
8. tilt

9. ellipse
10. axis
12. equator

DOWN

1. sphere
2. day
3. solstice
5. equinox

6. winter
7. rotation
11. summer

Earth's Satellite (page 108)

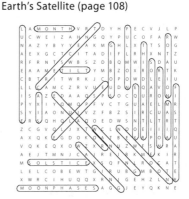

Earth's Satellite (page 109)

ACROSS

1. new moon
4. lunar eclipse
8. full moon

9. waxing
12. month
13. third quarter

DOWN

2. waning
3. maria
5. crescent
6. solar eclipse

7. first quarter
10. moon phases
11. gibbous

Sun-Earth-Moon System (page 110)

1. C
2. A
3. A and D or A and B

4. C
5. C

To the Moon! (page 111)

Answers will vary.

Solar and Lunar Eclipses (page 112)

1.–2.

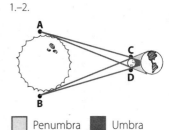

□ Penumbra ■ Umbra

Solar and Lunar Eclipses (continued)

3. solar eclipse
4. new moon
6. the umbra
7. Answers will vary.
8.–9.

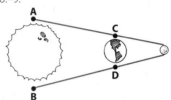

10. lunar eclipse
11. full moon
12. nighttime
13. The moon's orbit is not in the same plane as Earth's orbit around the sun, so the Earth and moon line up directly only a few times per year.
14. Mercury and Venus don't experience eclipses because they have no moons.
15. Answers will vary.

Modeling Moon Phases (page 114)

5.

First Quarter	Waxing Gibbous	Full Moon
Waning Gibbous	Third Quarter	Waning Crescent

6. solar eclipse
7. lunar eclipse

Our Solar System (page 115)

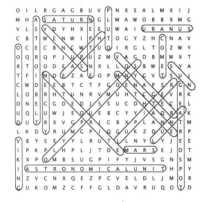

Inner Solar System (page 116)

ACROSS
3. Mars
5. asteroid belt
7. *Viking*
8. Olympus Mons

DOWN
1. Luna
2. Earth
3. Mercury
4. zero
6. sun
7. Venus

Outer Solar System (page 117)

ACROSS
3. Neptune
5. Oort cloud
6. Saturn
8. Great Red Spot

DOWN
1. Jupiter
2. Uranus
4. *Voyager*
7. methane
8. gas
9. Europa
10. Pluto

Solar System Distances (page 118)

Venus, 65.1 million miles, 0.7 AU
Earth, 93 million miles, 1.0 AU
Mars, 139.5 million miles, 1.5 AU
Jupiter, 483.6 million miles, 5.2 AU
Saturn, 883.5 million miles, 9.5 AU
Uranus, 1,785.6 million miles, 19.2 AU
Neptune, 2,790 million miles, 30.0 AU

Which Planet Am I? (page 119)

1. Mars
2. Venus
3. Uranus
4. Mercury
5. Earth
6. Jupiter
7. Earth
8. Venus
9. Mars
10. Neptune
11. Jupiter
12. Saturn
13. Saturn
14. Mercury
15. Neptune and Uranus

Planetary Missions (page 121)

1. A flyby involves sending a spacecraft past the planet, usually to take pictures on its way to another planet.

   An orbiter circles a planet or moon for an extended period of time, usually to map the surface or conduct other broad studies of the planet.

   Robotic landers actually land in a predetermined location to conduct an in-depth study of a certain area.

   Human missions allow highly in-depth studies of the planet or moon. They require complex mission planning and can be very dangerous

2. Answers will vary.
3. Answers will vary.
4. Answers will vary.
5. Answers will vary.
6. Answers will vary but may include:

Flyby
Advantage: can view many planets in the same mission
Disadvantage: limited data and information returned

Orbiter
Advantage: provides a broad view of an entire planet
Disadvantage: cannot do an in-depth study of a specific area

Robotic lander
Advantage: allows in-depth study of a small area
Disadvantage: complex mission with lots of opportunity for something to go wrong; can only observe a small area of a planet or moon

Human
Advantages: can collect samples; can provide decision-making skills to solve problems or answer questions
Disadvantages: highly complex mission; risky, very expensive

7. orbiter
8. lander
9. human/lander
10. orbiter
11. flyby
12. human
13. lander
14. orbiter